How to Write a Poem

How to Study Literature

The books in this series – all written by eminent scholars renowned for their teaching abilities – show students how to read, understand, write, and criticize literature. They provide the key skills which every student of literature must master, as well as offering a comprehensive introduction to the field itself.

Published

How to Write a Poem

John Redmond

Blackwell
Publishing

BLACKWELL PUBLISHING
350 Main Street, Malden, MA 02148-5020, USA
9600 Garsington Road, Oxford OX4 2DQ, UK
550 Swanston Street, Carlton, Victoria 3053, Australia

First published 2006 by Blackwell Publishing Ltd

2 2006

Library of Congress Cataloging-in-Publication Data

Redmond, John, 1967–
    How to write a poem / John Redmond.
        p. cm.—(How to study literature)
    Includes bibliographical references and index.
        ISBN-13: 978-1-4051-2479-9 (hard cover : alk. paper)
        ISBN-10: 1-4051-2479-2 (hard cover : alk. paper)
        ISBN-13: 978-1-4051-2480-5 (pbk. : alk. paper)
        ISBN-10: 1-4051-2480-6 (pbk. : alk. paper) 1. Poetry—Authorship.
    1. Title. II. Series.

    PN1059.A9. R43 2006
    808.1—dc22

                                          2005006596

A catalogue record for this title is available from the British Library.

Set in 10½/13pt Minion
by Graphicraft Ltd, Hong Kong

For further information on
Blackwell Publishing, visit our website:
www.blackwellpublishing.com

Contents

Acknowledgements

The editor and publisher gratefully acknowledge the permission granted to reproduce the copyright material in this book:

A. R. Ammons, 'Loss', from *Collected Poems 1951–1971* (New York: Norton, 1972). Copyright © 1972 by A. R. Ammons. Reprinted by permission of W. W. Norton & Company, Inc.

Gottfried Benn, 'Little Aster' and 'Night Café', from E. B. Ashton (ed.), *Primal Visions: Selected Writings of Gottfried Benn* (New York: New Directions, 1960). Copyright © 1971 by New Directions Publishing Corp. Reprinted by permission of New Directions Publishing Corp.

Elizabeth Bishop, 'Five Flights Up', from *Complete Poems* (London: Chatto, 1991). Copyright © 1979, 1983 by Alice Helen Methfessel. Reprinted by permission of Farrar, Straus and Giroux, LLC.

Charles Bukowski, 'My Old Man', from *Love is a Dog From Hell: Poems 1974–1977* (Santa Rosa: Black Sparrow Press, 1991). Copyright © 1991 by Charles Bukowski. Reprinted by permission of HarperCollins Publishers Inc.

Anne Carson, 'Quintia Formosast Multis', from *Men in the Off Hours* (New York: Knopf, 2000). Copyright © 2000 by Anne Carson. Reprinted by permission of Alfred A. Knopf, a division of Random House, Inc, and Jonathan Cape, a division of The Random House Group Ltd. Random House, Inc.

Ciaran Carson, 'Bloody Hand', from *Belfast Confetti* (Loughcrew: Gallery, 1989). Copyright © 1989 by Ciaran Carson. Reprinted by permission of the author, The Gallery Press and Wake Forest University Press.

Hans Magnus Enzensberger, 'Model Towards a Theory of Recognition', from *Selected Poems*, translated by Hans Magnus Enzensberger and Michael Hamburger (Newcastle: Bloodaxe, 1994). Copyright © 1994 by Hans Magnus Enzensberger and Michael Hamburger. Reprinted by permission of Suhrkamp Verlag.

Robert Frost, 'Come In' and 'Not to Keep', from Edward Connery Latham, *The Poetry of Robert Frost* (New York: Henry Holt, 1979). Copyright © 1923, 1969 by Henry Holt and Company, copyright © 1942, 1951 by Robert Frost, copyright © 1970 by Lesley Frost Ballantine. Reprinted by permission of Henry Holt and Company, LLC and The Rondom House Group Ltd.

David Gascoyne, 'The Very Image', from Robin Skelton, *Poetry of the Thirties* (London: Penguin, 1964). Copyright © 1964 by David Gascoyne. Reprinted by permission of The Estate of David Gascoyne.

Jorie Graham, 'Notes on the Reality of the Self' and 'What the End is For', from *The Dream of the Unified Field: Selected Poems* (Manchester: Carcanet, 1996). Copyright © 1995 by Jorie Graham. Reprinted by permission of HarperCollins Publishers Inc and Carcanet Press Limited.

W. S. Graham, 'Dear Bryan Wynter' and 'The Beast in Space', from *Selected Poems* (New York: Ecco, 1980). Copyright © 1980 by W. S. Graham. Reprinted by permission of The Estate of W. S. Graham.

Robert Graves, 'translation of Amergin', from *The White Goddess* (London: Faber & Faber, 1948). Copyright © 1948 by Robert Graves. Reprinted by permission of Carcanet Press Limited.

Miroslav Holub, 'Reading', from *Supposed to Fly*, Ewald Osers (Newcastle: Bloodaxe, 1996). Copyright © 1996 by Miroslav Holub. Reprinted by permission of Bloodaxe Books Ltd.

Kenneth Koch, 'To the Ohio', from *New Addresses* (New York: Knopf, 2001). Copyright © 2001 by Kenneth Koch. Reprinted by permission of the Kenneth Koch Literary Estate.

Michael Longley, 'Letter to Seamus Heaney', from *Selected Poems* (London: Jonathan Cape, 1998). Copyright © 1998 by Seamus Heaney. Reprinted by permission of The Random House Group Ltd and Wake Forest University Press.

C. H. Sisson, 'A Letter to John Donne', from *Collected Poems 1943–1982* (Manchester: Carcanet, 1984). Copyright © 1984 by C. H. Sisson. Reprinted by permission of Carcanet Press Limited.

Acknowledgements

Wislawa Szymborska, 'Funeral' and 'Pi', from *View with a Grain of Sand: Selected Poems* (London: Harvest, 1995). Copyright © 1993 by Wislawa Szymborska, English translation by Stanislaw Baranczak and Clare Cavanagh, copyright © 1995 by Harcourt, Inc. Reprinted by permission of the publisher.

C. K. Williams, 'Instinct', from *Selected Poems* (New York: Farrar, Straus and Giroux, 1995). Copyright © 1994 by C. K. Williams. Reprinted by permission of Farrar, Straus and Giroux, LLC and Bloodaxe Books Ltd.

C. D. Wright, 'Treatment', from *Steal Away: Selected and New Poems* (Port Townsend: Copper Canyon Press, 2002). Copyright © 2002 by Copper Canyon Press.

W. B. Yeats, 'Adam's Curse', 'The Fiddler of Dooney', 'To a Squirrel at Kyle-na-no' and 'Untitled poem', from *Collected Poems* (London: Macmillan, 1982). Copyright © 1982 by W. B. Yeats. Reprinted by permission of A. P. Watt Ltd.

Every effort has been made to trace copyright holders and to obtain their permission for the use of copyright material. The publisher apologizes for any errors or omissions in the above list and would be grateful if notified of any corrections that should be incorporated in future reprints or editions of this book.

Introduction

What is poetry? This seems like a good place to start. There is a word, 'poetry', so there must be – must there not? – something to which that word refers. When we sit down to write a poem we may think, *now, before I go any further I need to have a clear picture of what poetry is.* And once we have formed that picture, we may think, naturally enough, that any poem we construct should conform to it. While this line of thinking may seem clear and good, I think that it is misguided. I suggest that the question *What is poetry?* is an unhelpful one, especially for writers, and that there are two reasons for this. First, the question tempts us to think it has a definitive answer – it hasn't. Second, and more dangerously, it tempts us to think that it is but a step from knowing what poetry *really* is to writing real poetry.

A founding assumption of this book is that, far from being helpful, many popular ways of thinking about poetry are tremendous handicaps. By way of alternative, this book will encourage readers to focus on the promise and opportunity of the blank page. To focus on the *possibility* of writing poems I believe it is helpful to use definitions of poetry which are not couched in the present tense. Hence I want to set aside the distracting question of *what poetry is* and to replace it with two more helpful and more exciting questions: *what might poetry be?* And *what has poetry been?* For to think about poetry in terms of the future places an emphasis on *opportunity*, affirms that a poem may take a shape not assumed before, may not behave as other poems have behaved. To think about poetry in terms of the past places an emphasis on *exploration*, affirms that we can learn from the opportunities which previous poems have exploited. Both ways of thinking support another assumption of this book: that rather than turning our experiments with writing towards some definition of what poetry 'is', we do better to turn what we write towards the experiment of our lives.

Modern life is highly bureaucratized. We spend much of our lives conforming to structures – often very rigid ones – from traffic-lights to tax-codes, from 'move along' to 'mind the gap'. We may spend little of our time changing structures and even less of our time devising new ones. Bullied so often and so successfully, we may come to think of poetry as one more master to obey. We may ask ourselves, in deference to the poetic tradition, what exactly are the rules to be followed? To what principles must I submit? We may think of a career in poetry as dependent on a set of qualifications to be obtained, an exam to be passed, after suitable immersion in, and diligent adherence to, the Poetry Rulebook. It is easy to give structure too much respect, just as it is tempting to make ourselves comfortable with a new thing by squeezing it into an old set of structures. But to do this is to get things exactly the wrong way around. Rather than explore a life for its structure, we do better, as the American philosopher Ralph Waldo Emerson observed, to explore a structure for its life. Of course, to have a rulebook to read, a form to follow, a structure to observe, would make life easier. Rules are reassuring. Even experienced writers, when they produce something fresh and new, may be guilty of asking themselves, as if by reference to an imaginary rulebook, *yes, this is good but is it poetry?* It is hard not to seek reassurance, but there is no way to be reassured. For poetry does not have a nature.

To form a poem is to experiment with being, in other words, to have a personality. There is no final way to separate the activity of writing poetry from the kind of people we are, or want to be. The literary critic Randall Jarrell once compared the experience of reading the *Collected Poems* of Wallace Stevens to setting a man down on Mars and asking him to explore it. Similarly, any good poem should make us feel like explorers of a new planet, setting out on a momentous adventure. It should provoke us to ask 'Where am I?', 'What am I doing here?', 'Where might I be going next?' As much as possible, a good poem will try to maintain the openness, the sense of possibility, which every reader feels when they open a book for the first time. To write a poem is to create, or even to become, a new form of life. But that life will only be new when it has moved to separate itself from the formulae of poets, academics, and other literary commentators. Well known for rewriting his own poems, W. B. Yeats was clear what this process meant for his personality:

The friends that have it I do wrong
When ever I remake a song,
Should know what issue is at stake:
It is myself that I remake.[1]

To experiment with the literary future is also to explore the literary past. To think about what poetry *has been* is to recognize that new relationships arise out of old. To have a sense of what a poem might become we need to explore what different poems, at different times, became. We look at the past not in order to discover what is written in the 'Poetry Rulebook', but to make the whole idea of a Rulebook seem foolish. I want the reader to think about poetry's past always with respect to its future, in the spirit of Winston Churchill's remark, 'the further back I look, the further forward I can see'.

What poetry might be is up for grabs. There is nothing inevitable about what poems written in twenty years' time will look like. There is no ultimate venue where poetry is booked to appear. Therefore, the design of this book seeks to free potential writers from preconceived ideas of what is literary, what is properly poetic. It has been said that a writer is one who teaches their mind to misbehave. Readers of this book are encouraged, literally and metaphorically, to look at the world upside down, to have minds which misbehave. At the same time, I do not want to suggest that this is bound to be an easy process. To look at the world upside down may be disturbing. As the poet Paul Celan dryly observed, 'the man who walks on his head sees the sky below, as an abyss'.[2]

As will become clear, this book endorses a relational way of thinking about poetry. To put it another way, this book sees any poem, and the practice of writing poetry, as a continually rewoven set of relationships. My attachment to this view and my belief in its significance requires some explanation. New writers are often intimidated, puzzled, and in many ways put off, by poetry. Why? I think this is substantially because many of the popular ideas about poetry which are currently in circulation are deeply misleading and come between the writer and what they might write. So my attachment to a relational way of thinking about poetry is at once corrective and suggestive. Let me begin by focusing on three ways of thinking which I think unnecessarily burden writers old and new. These are (1) the set of ideas, mostly popular, which would like to mark poetry off as a radically separate activity; (2) the desire to read poetry in terms of absolutes which exist outside the poem, to which any poem is supposedly attached; (3) the desire to isolate something essential inside the poem which would justify its existence. What all of these ideas have in common is a desire to think about poetry in non-relational terms. After tackling these ideas, I will move on to offering my own relativistic account of writing poetry and explain the layout of the various chapters.

Most popular notions of poetry are derived from the period when poetry last had a wide general audience and real cultural sway: the nineteenth century. Say the word 'poet' to most people and the first person they are likely to think about is a Romantic poet, probably Wordsworth, Byron or Keats. Owing to a peculiar range of factors, which I do not intend to go into here, Romantic poetry of the nineteenth century, in recoil from scientific rationalism and the dehumanizing forms of social organization which followed the Industrial Revolution, conceived of poetry as a radically separate sphere of activity. According to the mythology which the Romantic poets cultivated, and which continues to have widespread general influence, the true poet is a creature regularly visited by something called 'Inspiration', the visits being especially frequent when the poet is in close proximity to 'Nature'. This image of the poet is much like the one described at the end of Coleridge's 'Kubla Khan':

> And all should cry, Beware! Beware!
> His flashing eyes, his floating hair!
> Weave a circle round him thrice,
> And close your eyes with holy dread,
> For he on honeydew hath fed,
> And drunk the milk of Paradise.

While this way of thinking about the figure of the poet is colourful – and that, after all, is why it is popular – it has a number of undesirable consequences. At heart it makes a misleading distinction between poetry and other things we make, from shoes to ships, from choral symphonies to computer games. We would not dream of describing an architect who has designed a beautiful house with the kind of language which Coleridge uses. Just as the image of the architect as a wild-eyed loon is an unnecessary mystification, so too with the image of the poet. Usually when a poet is asked – as they are often asked – from where do they draw their 'inspiration', the question assumes the validity of the nineteenth-century model. The problem with this assumption is that it overlooks the importance of work, unglamorous work which any good poet undertakes in various forms: observation, experiment, the creation of patterns of mind. Successful poems are, in general, not only the products of numerous drafts, they are also the products of deliberately cultivated habits of being (in this sense they are dependent on personality, which is after all a habit of being). Inspiration is just a colourful metaphor which we might now do better to discard. Even the word 'creativity' owes something to the influence of the nineteenth-century model. Although it is widely used in universities, most writers I suspect are uncomfortable with the phrase, 'Creative Writing'. Here is what Miroslav Holub, the great Czech poet (and leading immunologist), has to say about the term:

> I must state that I have never felt anything like creativity and, even if I had, I would not be caught dead admitting it. For me, 'creativity' is too luxurious a word, too richly coloured. What I know is the will for and the enjoyment of new things, and these are identical in science and art. I think scientific and artistic activities do not exclude one another, no matter how different their techniques are. It is all about energy or steam, all about transformations of energy.[3]

Rather than use a term like 'creativity', it might be better to use a term like 'design' and to think of poets as 'poetry designers'. 'Design' is a word which does not make us think of a marked-off, rarefied form of activity and, above all, the term has not lost its associations with hard work. The word 'creative' may make the writer seem like a Creator in an unreal sense, someone who is making something out of nothing, bringing something into existence where before there had only been a vacuum.

We are, in general, too apt to picture the writer as an isolated individual, and writing as a solitary activity. Certainly, for many stages of composition a writer is indeed on their own. Yet just as I think it is helpful to think of the poem as a web which is spun out of old webs so I think it better to conceive of writing as an act on behalf of a community, or – better – a series of interlocking communities. By writing we make a series of contracts: with past and present users of the English language, with the peer community which supports and criticizes our work, with publishers, editors and reviewers, and eventually with those readers we will never hear from or see.

In popular mythology, poetry is associated with misty absolutes – Freedom, Beauty, Truth, Soul, Inspiration. Sometimes poetry is turned into

5

'Poetry' and is given an honorary place alongside these exotic creatures. Why do these absolutes hold such sway? Essentially, because it is hard to think of poetry – or anything else we love – as mortal. To compensate for the vulnerability of the things we love, we bathe them in a glow of permanence. The kind of fixity we look for has been characterized by William James:

> Something to support the finite many, to tie it to, to unify and anchor it. Something unexposed to accident, something eternal and unalterable. The mutable in experience must be founded on immutability . . . This is the resting deep. We live upon the stormy surface; but with this our anchor holds, for it grapples rocky bottom. This is Wordsworth's 'central peace subsisting at the heart of endless agitation' . . . This is Reality with the big R, reality that makes the timeless claim, reality to which defeat can't happen.[4]

When we talk about 'the timeless spirit of Poetry', we invoke a reality to which defeat can't happen. This book takes the view that, if there is a 'reality to which defeat can't happen', then it has nothing to do with poetry. There is a wise African proverb which says that a person is a person through persons. In the same way an object is an object through objects, and a poem is a poem through poems. Any fragment of our experience can only be measured by reference to other fragments. As the American thinker Richard Rorty puts it, 'only about the relative is there anything to say'.[5]

As many writers will admit, probably the single best piece of advice to give a prospective author is to *show* rather than *tell* (this piece of advice is well known but that does not stop it from being good). Here is a brief illustration: Let us say we want to describe a character, called Bill, who is ugly. We can simply tell the reader that 'Bill is ugly.' But we could also *show* the reader that this is so with a description, for example, 'Bill has a face like a disappointed bulldog.' Now why should it be that showing works better than telling? Because showing is intensely relational while telling is not. When we show, we set in motion a potentially boundless set of relationships; when we tell we reduce the new to the old, to familiar types.

Absolutes like Truth, Beauty and Freedom (or for that matter Deceit, Ugliness and Slavery) swallow everything that is new and living. What can we say, for example, about the abstraction 'Love'? If we mean by it some absolute quality, or an intrinsic property, then we say nothing. If we love someone then the emotion must be performed in a concrete way – we shed tears or buy flowers or embrace. In the absence of such acts, whatever we mean by 'Love' will be invisible to others and an illusion to ourselves. By contrast everything that is genuinely new and living is an event and every event is a new relationship: the cat drops in my lap, the arrow strikes the target, the cuckoo flies the nest. And whatever is new in language is a new event in language. Think, for example, what happens when we bring together two words that are not used to each other's company. When we put donkey beside orange; octopus beside mirror; and windmill beside flamingo – we release a new energy. We experience a donkey in a different way when we think of it 'via' an orange and vice versa. Famously, the nineteenth-century French writer Lautreamont compared beauty to 'the chance encounter, on a dissecting table, of an umbrella and a sewing-machine'. Nothing like the same kind of tension is generated by placing the horse beside, or even before, the cart. On the other hand, we might release more imaginative energy if we place the horse *on top* of the cart.

Just as we often handicap ourselves by trying to yoke a particular poem to some overarching idea of what poetry is, so we may try to nail a poem down to something we pretend is inside it: its meaning. These manoeuvres are inner and outer manifestations of the same impulse, a desire to secure the poem to some permanent structure, to take away its fragile set of dependencies. As sparks fly up when flint meets rock, so meanings fly up when reader meets poem. Sparks are contained neither by flint nor by rocks but arise from their relationship. In the same way, meanings are contained neither by the reader nor by the poem but arise from their relationship. To adapt a phrase of the German philosopher Lichtenberg's, if an ass peers into a poem, you can't expect an apostle to look out. Poems do not *contain* meanings. There is nothing beneath, behind or inside a poem, just as there is nothing beneath, behind or inside the universe. There is no way to explain, justify or approve of a poem merely by reference to its meaning. As the literary critic Richard Poirier has put it, every reading experience is a struggle between what the reader wants to make of the book and what the book wants to make of the reader. When a poem, or any other art-work, is successful it is because it makes us 'better' (that is to say, it stimulates an experience which makes us more interesting, more nuanced, more many-sided, more flexible), not because of the rightness or nobility or bravery of its imagined meaning. Poems, like other experiences, may turn out to be good or bad but they cannot be right or wrong. Of course, we are inclined to believe that poems *do* have meanings because of the unfortunate ways we transmit poetry in our culture. Our first encounters with poetry are often at school and, in the end, school boils down to providing answers (or meanings) in response to exam questions. But the meaning of *Paradise Lost* is not *York Notes to Paradise Lost* (if such a thing exists). *Paradise Lost* does not have a meaning.

I want to turn from these ways of thinking about poetry which I think are unhelpful to ways I consider helpful. I want to start with the biggest picture first, the place which poetry occupies in human culture. Granted that poetry is about changing relationships which have already existed, what can we say about the kind of newness which I have already spoken about? What does it mean to talk about the promise and opportunity of the blank page? If poetry is necessarily related to its past, how can we find useful ways of thinking about what it might become in the future?

Emerson said that a man is never more himself than when he is getting out of his idea of himself. Now this may sound obscure, but the commonsense meaning of Emerson's suggestion is that we are most human when we are most open to change and, conversely, that we are least human when in the grip of habit or tradition, when we try to close down the possibilities of change. I want to sketch out a few ideas for how we might think of poetry with respect to the rest of our lives, offer some metaphors for how we might usefully think about newness, and in the process demystify a little what we are doing when we write a poem. John Lennon was once asked why the Beatles, in the mid-1960s, had embraced sitars, drugs and mysticism. By way of answer he said, 'Some people wanted us to be a bunch of moptops forever singing "I Feel Fine".' A writer who keeps repeating themselves is in the position of a pop-star always singing the same song. As W. H. Auden put it, as far as experimentalism goes, there are two issues: 'Every work of a writer should be a first step, but this will be a false step unless, whether or not he realize it at the time, it is also a further step.'[6] In cooking, to follow the advice of an expert closely – so closely that one reproduces their work exactly – may be a triumph. In poetry, it is a disaster. Successful poets produce their own recipes, and only use them once.

Let us think about writing poetry in the context of the general human desire for newness. What is it that makes us different from the animals? Why are we no longer huddling in caves or living up trees? Emerson believed that it was our desire *to go beyond ourselves* which truly distinguishes us from the animal. When our human ancestors were in caves, they presumably had, as gorillas and chimpanzees have, what is necessary to live, to get by. But our ancestors wanted something more, to go beyond the merely necessary. Hence, we began to experiment. It is our ability to create more than we need, our openness to the extra, from the DVD to the Taj Mahal, which distinguishes human beings. And all human culture – all our traditions, habits, cultural practices, all our buildings, poems and space-ships – was once, for someone somewhere, a new idea worked out in a concrete situation. As Richard Rorty sees it, civilization is a chain of new experiences which gradually harden into clichés and which are, in turn, refreshed by new experiences. One of the consequences of this view is that there is no privileged form of being, no special meaning, no misty abso-lute, no Key Which Unlocks All The Doors, that could exist outside this chain of making. All the flowers of culture, from the wheel to Wal-Mart, were created at some point. And all of them flourish or wither according to how much use we find for them. Another consequence of this view is that the person who regularly makes new things, like an artist or an inven-tor, assumes a special interest.

In the quest for newness, language has a special place, because language is the main tool we have for carving up reality – and each time we human beings carve up reality, from the smallest incision to the largest slice, it is in answer to a need, for without these needs we would not think to carve it in the first place. As human needs are as good as infinite, new uses of language, new metaphors, are demanded all the time. When these meta-phors arise, some succeed and some fail; some prove useful to the culture and some do not. This is how Rorty, following the philosopher Donald Davidson, invites us to think about metaphor. Rather than think of meta-phors as having a meaning, we do better to think of them in terms of familiar and unfamiliar uses of language. A metaphor remains a metaphor while it remains unfamiliar. When it becomes familiar then, in the view of Davidson and Rorty, it becomes literal. As Rorty puts it: 'Davidson lets us think of the history of language, and thus of culture, as Darwin taught us to think of the history of the coral reef. Old metaphors are constantly dying off into literalness, and then serving as a platform and foil for new metaphors.'[7]

Granted that we think about poetry in terms of newness, what is it that distinguishes one new poem from another? Does it serve any purpose to describe a poem as good or bad? The metaphor I would use to answer this is that the poet's position is analogous to that of someone who is designing a game, while the reader's position is analogous to that of some-one who is playing or watching the game. When one is designing a game, it is possible to vary the effects of playing the game without determining its outcome. The key is the difference between design and performance. For example, it is now common to see reviews of computer games in the mainstream media. These reviews effectively treat computer games as a form of art – they are not dissimilar to reviews of theatrical performances. Similarly, a poem is designed as an opportunity for the reader to perform it. As Auden said, 'a poem is, among other things, always a verbal game. Everybody knows that one cannot play a game without rules. One may make the rules what one likes, but one's whole fun and freedom comes from obeying them.'[8]

Let us take the game of baseball as an example. If baseball were to be redesigned, and if the distance between the bases were to be doubled, it would make it extremely difficult for a runner ever to reach first base. Many games played under these new rules would be scoreless. In other words, the performance would become less interesting. If we were to review this new version of baseball, in the way that a new computer game is reviewed, we would probably give it the thumbs down. Contrariwise, if one halved the distance between the bases, all games would be very high-scoring. It is likely that this new version of baseball would also get the thumbs down. As it is, baseball has been designed with a satisfying tension between the likelihood of the runner getting to first base and the likelihood of them being thrown out. An imperfect ground-ball gives the fielder just enough time to throw out a runner at first, but if the fielder makes a noticeable mistake, then such is the margin of error that the throwing-out of the runner becomes a doubtful proposition. There is a satisfying tension between success and failure.

None of these rules and designs, however, determines how any one game is played. No two games – no two plays – are the same, yet it remains the same game of baseball. Similarly, no two readings, no two performances of any poem are exactly the same, but it remains the same poem, the same order of marks on the page. When a poet writes a good poem, they are in the position of someone who designs a good game. Those who perform the well-designed poem or game are therefore likely to experience a range of satisfying balances and tensions.

To be able to design a game effectively, you need to know something about how people are likely to behave under certain conditions. The more you know about the probable behaviour of those taking part the better. This explains why the various constraints we impose on ourselves when writing a poem have a point. Every set of possibilities that we open closes another set. The same is true in reverse. Every set of possibilities we close opens another set. This is another way of saying that every time we press down on one part of the universe another part pops up. In this sense, as Auden said, form releases imagination. Any limitations, like the rules of baseball, are a potential source of interest, an invitation to improvise, to head off in new directions. As for the poet, the game-designer envisages tendencies, probable patterns, but never determines any one performance. And this is how we should think about freedom in a poem, roughly in the same way as we think about 'freedom' in a game. If the game becomes perfectly free, then it ceases to be of interest. So too with a poem.

Our predictions about how readers will react can be improved by reading other poems, but also by having more general experience of the world. Let me show how our relationships to the world affect the kind of predictions we make and relationships we trace within a poem. Certain forces and elements in the world – snow, water, fire – have a claim on our minds because we see them at work so often. Our minds become familiar with the kinds of relationship they trace. Because of this familiarity, these forces and elements appeal to poets. One good example is the wind. As the poet Ted Hughes observed: 'The wind, in all its phases, coming, here, going and gone, might be said to be one of the great subjects of poetry. Almost every poet, when he mentions the wind, touches one of his good moments in poetry.'[9] In part, this is because the action of the wind is dramatic. More crucially, this is because we have a considerable mental library devoted to the actions of the wind. Nearly every day, we see the wind acting upon something, and so our minds build up a deep reserve of thoughts and images. Therefore when we read about the wind acting in an otherwise unfamiliar situation, like *When Mr Smith crossed the road, the wind forced his umbrella inside out*, then it is not hard for our imaginations to come up with images that might fit this situation. Umbrellas, one might say, become more present to our minds – they exaggerate their 'umbrella-ness' – when open in the wind. Here is a further example: let us say I want to describe a man wearing a raincoat. I might animate this image by describing the man walking against the wind with his raincoat blowing about. I might then further animate the picture by inviting you to imagine the shadow of this man walking against the wind with his raincoat blowing about. In both cases we have an example of a set of relationships which is easy to imagine (all of us will provide different mental images for these examples, but the point is that the writer can be confident that such mental images are easily formed). In my imaginary picture, we see the wind act upon the man's coat and the

11

man's coat act upon the wind. After all, wind is only perceptible by virtue of what it does to the world – whether spinning a weather-vane or stealing a hat. Similarly, the creation of a shadow in the example above is thanks to the action of light imagined on the man and his coat. The shadow forms a set of relations – it grants us information about the man, the coat, the ground, the strength of the light, and so on.

Let us have a look at a poem where these observations of the work of shadow are put to use. The poem is by Thomas Campion:

Follow thy fair sun, unhappy shadow:
Though thou be black as night,
And she made all of light,
Yet follow thy fair sun, unhappy shadow.

Follow her whose light thy light depriveth.
Though here thou liv'st disgraced,
And she in heaven is placed,
Yet follow her whose light the world reviveth.

Follow those pure beams whose beauty burneth,
That so have scorchèd thee,
As thou still black must be,
Till her kind beams thy black to brightness turneth.

Follow her, while yet her glory shineth:
There comes a luckless night,
That will dim all her light;
And this the black unhappy shade divineth.

Follow still since so thy fates ordainèd:
The sun must have his shade,
Till both at once do fade,
The Sun still proved, the shadow still disdainèd.[10]

Let us dwell on Campion's poem for a moment. The poem is vivid because it immediately traces a relation, one that the imagination quickly seizes. If Campion had known of the existence of ultra-violet rays, would he have used them as readily as he used the play of shadow? Of course not, because even though ultra-violet rays surround us, so we are told, we do not see them in action very often. Campion could not rely on ultra-violet rays to create images in the reader's mind. Because he *could* rely on shadow, we can easily follow the progress of the central relationship, and at the same time follow the relationship between two people for which it stands, the tension between one who is happily loved and one who loves unhappily. More than likely, as we read the poem, we will feel that the poet identifies with the shadow, that the poet perhaps *is* the shadow, and that the poem amplifies something he feels, or has felt, for someone else. The poet develops the interdependence of sun and shadow by tracing its analogies with other situations. The relationship between light and dark is extended so that we are invited to think about life and death. Once the poem draws out one relationship, other relationships are able to form around it, in the way that one thread in a web supports others. Hence the relationship between light and shade extends another filament to the relationship between life and death. The poem also addresses the relationship between free will and fate. A shadow, in the natural world, has no choice but to follow the sun. But is that truly the case for someone who is in love? This question is close to the emotional heart of the poem, for the analogy between lover and shadow is not exact. Perhaps the poem does not resolve this point because it finds the question too painful. Certainly, its language and structure incline one to think that the speaker believes no choice is possible for the shadow. When we trace this particular strand of the poem's web, other strands – other relationships within the poem – modify it, make it more or less central, more or less weak. For example, the poem begins with an imperative verb, which it then repeats at the end of the first stanza and uses once more at the beginning of the second. Consequently, one has the sense of a mind compelled to act by something outside itself. This feeling of compulsion is deepened by the circular structure of those stanzas – each returns to the same line with which it began. The reader may choose to look for further shade in this apparently simple relationship, but the main point is that we can see how this vivid central web of the poem, and the simple natural observation from which it flows, allow other strands to be formed out of it.

Chapter Layout

The emphasis of this book is on ways of thinking about poetry, encouraging some and discouraging others. The various chapters amount to a set

13

of provisional themes which I hope develop the ways I wish to encourage in a suggestive manner. Each theme is illustrated by a number of poems and comes with an assignment. Let me make a disclaimer here. This book is not an account of specific writing practices – experiments with journal-keeping, automatic writing, twenty-minute exercises and the like – which are the steady diet of some creative writing courses. Although I recognize that some of these approaches provide structure for a course, I am agnostic about their value because they played no part in my own development as a writer. As far as writing *habits* go, I don't think any special advice is necessary beyond commonsense injunctions like write a lot, read a lot, observe a lot, revise a lot and be prepared to submit your work to others for criticism. Others may disagree, but rather than dwell on the value of this or that in-class exercise, I prefer to raise the reader's eyes to the possibilities of a poem.

The categories examined in the separate chapters are by no means supposed to be definitive. As I hope this introduction makes clear, I do not think that there is one right way to compose a poem. My approach in this book is to explore categories which are in themselves fresh and, to a degree, surprising. I have sought to avoid the kind of automatic chapters (for example, on the sonnet or the sestina) which one sometimes finds in books of this sort. This book is not intended to be a disguised guide to poetry in English. The reader will find other books which deal with topics like prosody and literary history elsewhere.

Part of my reason for exploring these suggestive categories is my conviction that most people can attain a level of technical competence in writing poetry quite easily. But technical competence is not in my view a sufficient condition for writing poetry well. What is more likely to make poems seem warped and shrunken is narrowness of outlook, even narrowness of personality. Technical competence is, unfortunately, easier to achieve than a flexible broad-mindedness. It is that kind of broad-mindedness which this book looks to encourage. In chapter 4, for example, I look at the non-traditional category of scale to make the reader think about issues of size and proportion – the whole idea of letting something small like a poem stand for something large like the world. This chapter is meant to be of practical use, but also meant to encourage new thinking, to help the reader think about what poetry might be in fresh ways.

The first three chapters are devoted to the first questions of poetic construction – who is speaking and to whom? where is the speaker located? and why does their speaking take this form? These chapters aim to discourage what I call the 'default contemporary poem': a poem with an 'I-persona' revealing the speaker's state of mind in a mostly conversational voice in a recognizable location. Against this model, I propose provocative, contrasting possibilities: Instead of an I-persona, for example, I encourage readers to try a 'we-persona' expressive, perhaps, of multiple states of mind; instead of a conversational voice, encourage them to try a parodic, or a deliberately exaggerated voice; instead of a morose tone, a tone of praise (perhaps in the form of an ode); instead of a recognizable location, a psychologized or surreal landscape.

Some categories which a reader would expect to find in a book of this sort are treated in a slightly unusual way. Instead of treating 'rhythm' as a separate topic, for example, I have decided to link it to the two chapters on line-length. This is for two reasons. First, I want readers to think about rhythm in a pragmatic way, in relation to one of the primary vehicles for writing poetry: the line-break. Second, I do not want to throw technical terms like 'iambic tetrameter' at the reader in a context divorced from practical writing. While it is useful to be familiar with technical terms, I do not think there is much point in fetishizing them. As the book develops, the various chapters specifically focus on issues like syntax and diction which a poet cannot reasonably avoid. Towards the end of the book, I introduce the reader to two traditional forms which stand in for how I see a poet might deal with the traditional canon and in what way a poet might employ old models. The final chapter on variety invites the reader to draw the examples of the book together, to think of the different categories in relation to each other, with reference to a single outstanding poem (by Jorie Graham).

Let me make one further disclaimer. As an Irish poet, who has lived in Britain for many years, and who has taught creative writing in the United States, I might reasonably be suspected of an allegiance to one national scene or another, or to one version of poetry as currently practised in one of these countries. I have no such allegiance and this book is very far from being a work of propaganda on behalf of any writing ideology. It is not an intervention in the various debates which would pit American poetry against British, academic poetry against mainstream, and postmodern poetry against the rest. While the reader may detect some patterns in those poems I have chosen as models, I hope those patterns are open and, broadly speaking, democratic. I have included a reasonable balance of poems from Britain, Ireland and North America, representative of various modes and periods, plus a fair sprinkling of translated works. The aim is not to please everybody but to give a sense of what is possible. If this book is anything, I hope it is a helpful signpost to a brighter poetic future. As Emerson said, the arts are initial not final. It is not what they achieve, it is what they aim at that matters. And if I might be permitted one concluding quotation, which might sum up the attitude of this book, it is this saying of George Santayana's: 'Art, like life, should be free, since both are experimental.'[11]

Notes

1   Peter Allt, ed., *The Variorum Edition of the Poems of W. B. Yeats* (New York: Macmillan, 1957), p. 778.
2   Paul Celan, *Collected Prose* (Manchester: Carcanet, 1986), p. 46.
3   Miroslav Holub, 'Poetry and Science', in *The Dimension of the Present Moment and Other Essays* (London: Faber, 1990), pp. 122–46: p. 118.
4   William James, 'Pragmatism and Humanism', Lecture 7 in *Pragmatism: A New Name for Some Old Ways of Thinking* (New York: Longman Green, 1907), pp. 92–104: p. 101.
5   Richard Rorty, *Truth and Progress: Philosophical Papers, Vol. 3* (Cambridge: Cambridge University Press, 1998), p. 3.
6   W. H. Auden, 'Writing', in *Selected Essays* (London: Faber, 1964), pp. 21–38: p. 31.
7   Richard Rorty, *Contingency, Irony and Solidarity* (Cambridge: Cambridge University Press, 1989), p. 16.
8   W. H. Auden, quoted in *Agenda* 10 (4)/11 (5) [double issue] 1972–3, p. 9.
9   Ted Hughes, *Poetry in the Making* (London: Faber, 1967), p. 33.
10 Helen Gardner, ed., *The New Oxford Book of English Verse 1250–1950* (Oxford: Clarendon Press, 1972), pp. 158–9.
11 George Santayana, *Reason in Art*, 1st edn. 1905 (New York: Collier, 1962), p. 122.

1

The Question of Address

In this opening chapter, I want to consider one of the most prominent features of what I call the 'default poem', first-person narration, and to suggest some provocative ways to avoid it. To whom, or to what, is the poem addressed – and who or what is doing the addressing? The question is not one we often think about. Many poems fall back on a simple lyric formula: an 'I-persona' describing its state of mind and feeling as though chatting with the reader across a coffee-table. Such poems might carry the invisible preface *I am a poet and this is how I feel right now*. The poem is passed from producer (writer) to consumer (reader) with all the transparency of a dollar bill. This is not surprising. We live in a confessional culture, a culture which puts a high value on frank self-expression, on the testimonies of eye-witnesses and the traumas of chat-show guests. In such a context the poem comes under pressure to be a field of self-display, a channel for colourful autobiography.

There is nothing inherently wrong with writing a poem in the form of a personal statement, because there is nothing inherently wrong with writing a poem in *any* form. The popularity of the default mode, however, should not blind us to other possibilities. It is also possible to think of all parties to this typical transaction – writer, poem, reader – as fictions. A poem need not pretend to be a sort of lace curtain behind which the spirit of the author flutters. Nor need it pretend that it is addressed to any particular individual. These are just conventions – useful at times – but conventions we can live without. A poem can represent a collective voice, a 'we', just as successfully as it can represent an individual voice, an 'I'. A poem can be the voice of an inanimate object – a rock, a cloud, the Statue of Liberty – just as much as it can be the voice of a person. It can be directed to a listener who is known to the speaker, just as much as it can be directed to an unknown listener. The speaker can even address themselves. In the course of this chapter I am going to look at some examples of unusual treatment of the speaker and the listener. Let us begin with an example drawn from the sixth century, credited to the mythological Irish poet Amergin:

> I am a stag: *of seven tines,*
> I am a flood: *across a plain,*
> I am a wind: *on a deep lake,*
> I am a tear: *the Sun lets fall,*
> I am a hawk: *above the cliff,*
> I am a thorn: *beneath the nail,*
> I am a wonder: *among flowers,*
> I am a wizard: *who but I*
> *Sets the cool head aflame with smoke?*
>
> I am a spear: *that roars for blood,*
> I am a salmon: *in a pool,*
> I am a lure: *from paradise*
> I am a hill: *where poets walk,*
> I am a boar: *ruthless and red,*
> I am a breaker: *threatening doom,*
> I am a tide: *that drags to death,*
> I am an infant: *who but I*
> *Peeps from the unhewn dolmen arch?*
>
> I am the womb: *of every holt,*
> I am the blaze: *on every hill,*
> I am the queen: *of every hive,*
> I am the shield: *for every head,*
> I am the tomb: *of every hope*[1]

The poem shows us that complex treatments of identity are a very old feature of Western culture. Not only is the 'I' detached from the identity of the writer, it is detached from the identity of any single speaker. The poem has something of a riddle-like quality, as if it were inviting us to solve the question 'Who am I?' or 'What am I?' The transformations which the mythical speaker undergoes are swift and enjoyable in themselves, but this is not how the main energy of the poem is generated. What principally effects us is the way in which the standard relationship between the 'I' and a stable speaking character has been thrown into question. After enjoying the imaginative energy of the rapid changes, we reflect on the poem and ask what is meant by using the phrase 'I am'. Why do 'we' think that the word 'I' can stand for something as fragile as a personality and, conversely, what do we think it can *not* stand for? (When we contemplate the various guises that the 'I' here adopts we may think that a number of them are inappropriate or illogical.)

A further consideration is that the word 'I' here may – without much stretching – come to stand for the poem itself, for the poem as a personality. Now this may seem fanciful – poems are not human beings, but like human beings they are affairs of language. Both are webs of words. In the absence of language, we can come to grips neither with a poem nor with a person. We notice that the 'I' of the poem does not 'protest' when it is attached to so many unlikely creatures and objects. Like language, human beings are awash with possibility, with the potential for being newly described, and all possibilities of this sort imply change. This is one way of saying that, at heart, this poem celebrates the power to change.

In our next example, Whitman's poem 'To You', the normal contract between the pronoun and the addressee is again disturbed. The poem begins with a phrase which is odd in itself 'Whoever you are' – a daring beginning. It suggests an intention to address the solitary but unknowable reader of the poem. As the poem progresses, however, it soon becomes apparent that Whitman is not addressing a single individual, or even a recognizable small group of individuals. The vagueness of the opening phrase assumes more point. We might say that Whitman does not know the 'you' he is addressing but that he does know it is *not* an individual. Here is the opening half of the poem:

Whoever you are, I fear you are walking the walk of dreams,
I fear these supposed realities are to melt from under your feet and hands,
Even now your features, joys, speech, house, trade, manners, troubles,
    follies, costume, crimes, dissipate away from you,
Your true body and soul appear before me,
They stand forth out of affairs, out of commerce, shops, work, farms,
    clothes, the house, buying, selling, eating, drinking, suffering, dying.

Whoever you are, now I place my hand upon you, that you be my poem,
I whisper with my lips close to your ear,
I have loved many women and men, but I love none better than you.

O I have been dilatory and dumb,
I should have made my way straight to you long ago,
I should have blabb'd nothing but you, I should have chanted nothing
    but you.

I will leave all and come and make the hymns of you,
None has understood you, but I understand you,
None has done justice to you, you have not done justice to yourself,
None but has found you imperfect, I only find no imperfection in you,
None but would subordinate you, I only am he who will never consent to
    subordinate you,
I only am he who places over you no master, owner, better, God, beyond
    what waits intrinsically in yourself.

Painters have painted their swarming groups and the centre-figure of all,
From the head of the centre-figure spreading a nimbus of gold-color'd
    light,
But I paint myriads of heads, but paint no head without its nimbus of
    gold-color'd light,
From my hand from the brain of every man and woman it streams,
    effulgently flowing forever.[2]

It is after the third line that we start to wonder about the kind of 'you'
Whitman is addressing. The list of categories which he wants to apply to
the 'you' would seem appropriate for a collective but not for one person.
On reflection, it would seem that Whitman wants the 'you' to stand for
something like humankind. The 'I' by contrast stands in a fairly conventional way for the speaker of the poem, Whitman himself. But even this
'I' has been made unstable by the change which has occurred in relation
to the 'you'. Now we are encountering an 'I' which is capable of having a
whole set of relationships with a collective 'you'. Who is this 'I' who is able
to pursue humankind, and what would such a pursuit entail?

By complicating the nature of the one addressed, Whitman has also complicated the position of the speaker. One of the consequences of this is that
actions, which would otherwise hardly be worthy of comment, draw more
attention to themselves. In lines 6 and 7, for example, Whitman describes
actions which would be banal in the context of an address to a single speaker.
In a love poem, it is very commonplace to whisper into the ear of another.
But this banality takes on a new appearance when one tries to imagine the
speaker whispering into the *ear* – rather than the ears – of a collective. While

this variation on a common motif is slight, the results are disproportionately effective.

This unusual use of address would seem merely tricksy if it did not somehow fit in with the overall direction of the poem. Whitman likes to conceive of human beings as part of a larger whole, as threads in a complicated fabric. Because he conceives of human personality and humankind as plural, the word 'you' is never merely singular. Both Amergin and Whitman complicate the positions of speaker and reader but we nevertheless feel that they are addressing human beings. It need not always be so. As the next poem demonstrates, we can also use the pronoun 'you' to address that which is not human, or not even living.

In Kenneth Koch's 'To the Ohio', the pronoun 'you' is used to address a river. In this poem, there is no question of the speaker addressing the reader – rather the reader is in the position of a third party overhearing a conversation between the poet and his beloved river. The effect is energetic and comic. Koch's style is well known for being good-humoured and unpretentious yet at the same time intelligent and moving:

To the Ohio

You separated my hometown from Kentucky
And south of us you deftly touched Indiana. Ohioans drove back over
     you
With lower-priced (untaxed) beer and Bourbon in the trunks
Of their cars to take to Cincinnati and get drunk
Less expensively than with Ohio purchases. In my teenage years
I drove over you in the other direction – to Campbell County –
To gamble, to the Hotel Licking to look at the pretty young prostitutes,
     and drink six-point-seven-percent Hudepohl Beer.
Your heyday had come when I was ten. We were down in the basement
To see if you were there yet. You flooded! You overflowed your banks!
Everything was wet
For miles around you. You were in the papers, trees stood in you up to
     their faces.
Men rowed
Boats from one side of a street to another. Doctors
Ran around the city giving typhoid shots. I kept a scrapbook
A big one, of newspaper coverage of you
That was so much admired for its pasted-on white and pink clippings
I was happy about it for a month.

You reappeared beneath the *Island Queen* – five years later –
Which steamed up you to an amusement park – Coney Island,
Named after the one in New York – with Kentucky on your other side.
Leaning over the rail, I looked at it and you, a muddy divider
Between wild good times and the regular life, Kentucky and Ohio –
From one you took your name, and from the other, then, your meaning.[3]

There are many ways of stretching the use of the word 'you' in a poem. One way is to address objects which can talk back, another way is to address objects which cannot. If we feel that the addressee is capable of an answer, then we may expect to hear it. Whitman uses 'you' in an unusual way, but is still addressing a human collective which can register that he is talking to them. The river in this poem cannot recognize that it is being praised. So why address something which cannot answer back? One way to answer this is to consider what would happen if the subject of the poem, the poet's memory of the Ohio, were to be tackled in a more conventional way. In that case, the poet would continue to speak in the first person but the river would be referred to in the third person, probably as an 'it'. Would anything be lost – or gained – as a result?

Most probably the first thing we would notice would be a change in mood. The poem would lose immediacy. By engaging in an imaginary conversation with the river Koch brings it closer – both to speaker and to reader. A conversational format is nearly always dramatic, partly because it leaves possibilities open – the possibility of receiving a reply, of changing one's mind, of being interrupted or challenged. When Koch addresses the river, the reader has to imagine a kind of space where such an interchange is possible, has to imagine the river as a kind of personality, sitting across the coffee-table, if you like, from the speaker.

Such anthropomorphic processes may seem childish, but they fulfil very old human impulses. As the ancient Greek philosopher Thales had it: there are gods in all things. To give inanimate objects a personality is to perform the same kind of imaginative process as we do with human beings, for personality is itself only a metaphor. Koch inverts the metaphor of personality by applying it to a river because the same feelings of love and respect which give rise to our desire to 'personalize' human beings are operating in this case. The river has become a kind of person to him. It has taken part in many of the dramas of his life and – as his list of the differences between Kentucky and Ohio demonstrates – it has come to stand, or flow, for certain values in his mind.

The last poem I want to look at in this chapter is a slightly more complicated example of what happens when one tampers with the default fiction of the poem. In 'The Beast in the Space', the Scottish poet W. S. Graham dramatizes the positions of speaker and reader in a consciously offbeat way.

THE BEAST IN THE SPACE

Shut up. Shut up. There's nobody here.
If you think you hear somebody knocking
On the other side of the words, pay
No attention. It will be only
The great creature that thumps its tail
On silence on the other side.
If you do not even hear that
I'll give the beast a quick skelp
And through Art you'll hear it yelp.

The beast that lives on silence takes
Its bite out of either side.
It pads and sniffs between us. Now
It comes and laps my meaning up.
Call it over. Call it across
This curious necessary space.
Get off, you terrible inhabiter
Of silence. I'll not have it. Get
Away to whoever it is will have you.

He's gone and if he's gone to you
That's fair enough. For on this side
Of the words it's late. The heavy moth
Bangs on the pane. The whole house
Is sleeping and I remember
I am not here, only the space
I sent the terrible beast across.
Watch. He bites. Listen gently
To any song he snorts or growls
And give him food. He means neither
Well or ill towards you. Above
All, shut up. Give him your love.[4]

In this, and in many other of his poems, Graham tries to grapple with the shortcomings of language as a means of genuine expression. Throughout his work he exhibits a keen sense of how often, and by how much, his

23

words fall short. 'The Beast in the Space' dramatizes the reader as a 'you' about to be visited by a very strange creature indeed. If we compare Graham's poem to Whitman's 'To You', we immediately notice the isolated nature of Graham's addressee. Graham pictures his reader as a lonely individual whereas Whitman seems to be addressing a whole people. The sense of loneliness in Graham's poem is enhanced by atmospheric details: the hour is late, the house is quiet, the setting is bare, and underneath everything, the poet says, is a silence ready to swallow him up.

To address the reader directly, and so draw attention to the artificiality of the poem as a means of communication, is a relatively common technique. Graham complicates it in two ways. First, he makes us believe that the writing of the poem is taking place almost at the same time as the receiving: the transmission of words from writer to reader has the near-immediacy of a phone-call and this naturally heightens the drama of the situation. Second, and more importantly, he uses the second-person pronoun to address the strange beast which he claims is roving back and forth between writer and reader. This is a serious poem, but it contains a number of comic touches and most of these are visible when he addresses this cat-like creature. The poem is in an imperative mood ('Shut up. Shut up') which sounds like someone addressing an awkward adult or perhaps a child. This brusque form of address is mirrored by the way in which the speaker addresses the beast, creating an uneasy equivalence. Both addresses contribute to the image of a grumpy, exasperated speaker who has entered into a rather reluctant relationship with the reader.

While it remains intensely faithful to the hope of full communication, Graham's poem is true to our habitual falling-short in language – his words seem to crumble under him. After all, viewed from one perspective, all we know is that the speaker is talking to himself. He receives no reply, from beast or reader. The poem leaves us with the vivid image of a man alone in his room, desperate to communicate, railing at the surrounding empty space, and shouting in frustration at phantom entities. At the same time, we have the poem which has brought this disturbing image 'over' to us, and we have a sense of a presence in the poem which is after all not far removed from the beast which the poem has described. The silence which the poet has evoked is there at the ends of the stanzas and at the end of the poem, flowing as a ghostly presence beneath it. Graham treats his own poem in this highly unusual way, noticeably complicating the patterns of address, and succeeds through its technique in leaving an eerie after-image in the reader's mind.

Your assignment is to write a poem which plays with the fiction of a writer addressing a reader. Here are some ideas: you might want to use the pronoun 'we' throughout, or pretend to be unsure the reader is there, or to address the poem to something – a tree, or a football stadium – which is not certain to respond.

Notes

1   Trans. Robert Graves, quoted in Robert Graves, *The White Goddess* (London: Faber, 1948), pp. 10–11.
2   Walt Whitman, *Poetry and Prose* (New York: Library of America College Editions, 1996), pp. 375–6.
3   Kenneth Koch, *New Addresses* (New York: Knopf, 2001).
4   W. S. Graham, *Selected Poems* (New York: Ecco, 1980), p. 35.

2

Viewpoint

The last chapter invited the reader to think about the ways in which the relationship between speaker and reader can be complicated. In this chapter I again want us to think about the relationship between where the speaker is looking from, the poem's viewpoint, and what the speaker is looking at, or thinking about. It can be helpful, for example, to think of a poem's point of view in terms of camera-shots. Sometimes we may usefully describe a poem as 'cinematic', meaning that it seems to follow cinema conventions in the sequence of its scenes and images. Ironically, such cinematic conventions developed in the first place from literary traditions. In this chapter, for example, we see how Thomas Hardy's 'Wessex Heights', which was written before the development of cinema, opens with what one might call an establishing shot, then zooms in on the speaker. It is a poem of long landscape shots, adopting at times what we might call the bird's-eye point of view. The posture implies that the speaker's position is privileged, that the poet *sees* a great deal, is specially gifted, perhaps even godlike. A viewpoint of this sort can be very effective when the poet wants to make large statements about society. As some examples in this chapter illustrate, English poets of the 1930s (who were much minded to offer social diagnoses) made extensive use of the bird's-eye point of view.

A poem can derive much, or even all, of its energy from the angles of view which it adopts, especially if it assumes numerous different ones. The poem by C. Day Lewis included here, for example, offers us a large number of perspectives in quick succession. Indeed much of the metaphorical effort in that poem is spent in forcing the reader to adopt as many of these as possible. A further effect, more obvious in the work of recent poets like C. D. Wright, is produced by deliberately playing on the relationship between the poem and an explicitly cinematic point of view. Such works draw self-consciously on the conventions of cinema. This is most obvious in the Wright poem because it uses the conceit of the film script.

Our first example is 'Wessex Heights' by Hardy:

There are some heights in Wessex, shaped as if by a kindly hand
For thinking, dreaming, dying on, and at crises when I stand,
Say, on Ingpen Beacon eastward, or on Wylls-Neck westwardly,
I seem where I was before my birth, and after death may be.

In the lowlands I have no comrade, not even the lone man's friend –
Her who suffereth long and is kind; accepts what he is too weak to mend:
Down there they are dubious and askance; there nobody thinks as I,
But mind-chains do not clank where one's next neighbour is the sky.

In the towns I am tracked by phantoms having weird detective ways –
Shadows of beings who fellowed with myself of earlier days:
They hang about at places, and they say harsh heavy things –
Men with a wintry sneer, and women with tart disparagings.

Down there I seem to be false to myself, my simple self that was,
And is not now, and I see him watching, wondering what crass cause
Can have merged him into such a strange continuator as this,
Who yet has something in common with himself, my chrysalis.

I cannot go to the great grey Plain; there's a figure against the moon,
Nobody sees it but I, and it makes my breast beat out of tune;
I cannot go to the tall-spired town, being barred by the forms now passed
For everybody but me, in whose long vision they stand there fast.

There's a ghost at Yell'ham Bottom chiding loud at the fall of night,
There's a ghost in Froom-side Vale, thin-lipped and vague, in a shroud of
     white,
There is one in the railway train whenever I do not want it near,
I see its profile against the pane, saying what I would not hear.

As for one rare fair woman, I am now but a thought of hers,
I enter her mind and another thought succeeds me that she prefers;
Yet my love for her in its fulness she herself even did not know;
Well, time cures hearts of tenderness, and now I can let her go.

So I am found on Ingpen Beacon, or on Wylls-Neck to the west,
Or else on homely Bulbarrow, or little Pilsdon Crest,
Where men have never cared to haunt, nor women have walked with me,
And ghosts then keep their distance; and I know some liberty.[1]

It is no exaggeration to claim that the entire poem is built around the speaker's viewpoint. The speaker of the poem is at pains to point out that, in response to changes of location, he has noticeably different kinds of thought. More than that, he suggests that according to where he stands – on the heights or on the plain, in the town or in the countryside – he is a *different kind of person*. So powerful is this realization that the speaker dramatizes it with an act of self-splitting, claiming to see himself in out-of-body fashion.

We might reflect on this for a moment. Is Hardy merely advancing a fanciful idea about the effect of point of view, or is there something in what he says which might help us to understand ourselves? Hardy reminds us about the relational nature of the self – we are indeed different kinds of person when we are placed in different environments. One of the reasons why we enjoy being outdoors 'in nature' – quite apart from scenic beauty – is because we place ourselves (if we are city-dwellers) in a radically different context, removing some relations while restoring others. Natural environments, for example, are usually free of other people, especially of the kind of people we might not choose to be with.

Many readers will feel some sense of identification with the speaker of Hardy's lines. For which of us does not feel misunderstood by others? Which of us does not like to feel that we have been thwarted by ghosts from our past? Which of us does not like to imagine ourselves, from time to time, removed from the crowd looking down at toiling humanity? I suspect a lot of readers will not just sympathize with the speaker of Hardy's poem, they will positively identify with it, because of the special point of view which it opens. Granted that one of the beguiling features of the poem is the way in which it invites us to occupy a viewpoint removed from humanity, one could go on to argue that this is something which quite a large number of poems do. They invite us to occupy a remote position, a thoughtful position above or beyond the crowd. This is particularly the case with poetry of the Romantic tradition, and one of the reasons why Romantic poetry remains attractive to many.

On close inspection, 'Wessex Heights' is not an entirely successful poem. Indeed the best parts of it are those explicitly associated with the elevated viewpoint. Throughout the rest of the poem, where Hardy dwells on his experiences at 'ground level', the poem uses hackneyed language and is much less memorable. But the good parts of the poem, principally the first and last stanzas, are very strong and cause such a reaction in most readers that the rest, I suspect, is forgiven. Part of the charm of these heightened viewpoints is the way in which they are combined with attractive place-names. Not only can we fantasize about looking down on everybody else, we can also imagine ourselves living in this colourful rural environment.

We might helpfully compare the effects of this poem, and learn how they can be used, by watching what W. H. Auden does when he adopts Hardy as a model. This is the opening stanza of the poem, 'Here on the cropped grass':

> Here on the cropped grass of the narrow ridge I stand,
> A fathom of earth, alive in air,
> Aloof as an admiral on the old rocks,
>   England below me:
> Eastward across the Midland plains
> An express is leaving for a sailors' country;
>   Westward is Wales
> Where on clear evenings the retired and rich
> From the french windows of their sheltered mansions
> See the Sugarloaf standing, an upright sentinel
>   Over Abergavenny.[2]

One can see that some of the effects here are very similar to those created by the Hardy poem. Auden's poem is more of a social and political critique, but the excitement generated by the elevated viewpoint is similar. For a start, the poem is immediately dramatic. It allows the poet to draw together activities which would otherwise be widely separated. And it tends to give to the speaker's voice a certain air of authority. As Hardy does, Auden uses proper names deliberately and with a certain obvious relish. Both poems propel themselves forward with an urgent rhythm to add to the sense of excitement and consequence.

The line of influence which one can trace from Thomas Hardy to W. H. Auden can be extended to C. Day Lewis. His poem 'The Magnetic Mountain' is typical of the 1930s social commentary school in England. Young, politically motivated poets, following Auden's example, were quick to use poetry to diagnose the social and political ills of English society. In pursuit of this goal, many of them used the elevated point of view. Here is an excerpt from 'The Magnetic Mountain':

You that love England, who have an ear for her music,
The slow movement of clouds in benediction,
Clear arias of light thrilling over her uplands,
Over the chords of summer sustained peacefully;
Ceaseless the leaves' counterpoint in a west wind lively,
Blossom and river rippling loveliest allegro,
And the storms of wood strings brass at year's finale:
Listen. Can you not hear the entrance of a new theme?

You who go out alone, on tandem or on pillion,
Down arterial roads riding in April,
Or sad beside lakes where hill-slopes are reflected
Making fires of leaves, your high hopes fallen:
Cyclists and hikers in company, day excursionists,
Refugees from cursed towns and devastated areas:
Know you seek a new world, a saviour to establish
Long-lost kinship and restore the blood's fulfilment.

You who like peace, good sorts, happy in a small way
Watching birds or playing cricket with schoolboys,
Who pay for drinks all round, whom disaster chose not;
Yet passing derelict mills and barns roof-rent
Where despair has burnt itself out – hearts at a standstill,
Who suffer loss, aware of lowered vitality;
We can tell you a secret, offer a tonic; only
Submit to the visiting angel, the strange new healer.

You above all who have come to the far end, victims
Of a run-down machine, who can bear it no longer;
Whether in easy chairs chafing at impotence
Or against hunger, bullies and spies preserving
The nerve for action, the spark of indignation –
Need fight in the dark no more, you know your enemies.
You shall be leaders when zero hour is signalled,
Wielders of power and welders of a new world.[3]

The opening of the poem invites us to contemplate a broad picture, a deep, soft-focus survey of the majestic English landscape. The elevated point of view is quickly suggested by words like 'clouds' and 'uplands'. Indeed the speaker could be occupying the very same position as the speaker in either the Hardy or the Auden poem. Nevertheless the speaker does not specify that they are standing on the side of a mountain, so the reader must imagine the point of view as being one of generalized elevation, a sort of floating bird's-eye view.

This is not a very subtle poem. As in 'Wessex Heights' what we respond to here is a primitive sense of excitement, the invitation to look down at a sick society as if we were gods, and in particular the vague sense of revolutionary uplift, the feeling that we are part of some new age on the verge of fruition. The vagueness of the poem's message is illustrated by phrases like 'the blood's fulfilment' and 'welders of a new world'. These phrases sound vaguely thrilling – who would not want to be on the side of something called 'the blood's fulfilment' – but the message is not at all focused; it is really little more than an example of the kind of rhetoric fashionable at the time. One notes, too, how the poet's initial elevation, and his subsequent materialization at a multitude of scenes, have encouraged him to adopt a hectoring tone, a tone of voice common in 1930s poetry, but one which we may struggle to find attractive now. This does not mean that the poem is worthless. There are aspects of it which we can admire just as we can admire, say, the cinematography of a film which, in other respects, we dislike.

Day Lewis's poem alerts us to the value of a decisively realized point of view – one which is definitely very obvious in setting the tone and mood of the poem. But his poem also alerts us to the value of changing points of view, sometimes very rapidly. We might say that any point of view implies a presence, implies that someone or something is there to do the viewing. Naturally, the reader is the one who is most likely to place themselves inside that viewpoint, so to change points of view rapidly is in a sense to shift the reader around quickly, almost in the manner of a physical workout. It may be to place the reader in a pleasant position, as in the aerial views we have just been studying, or it may be to place the reader, no less effectively, in a negative position. This is what happens in Gottfried Benn's 'Night Café':

824: The Love and Life of Women.
The 'cello has a quick drink. The flute
belches throughout three beats: oh, lovely sunset.
The drum reads on to the end of the thriller.

Green teeth, pimples in his face,
waves to conjunctivitis.

Grease in his hair
Talks to open mouth with swollen tonsils,
faith hope and charity around his neck.

Young goitre is sweet on saddle-nose.
He treats her to three beers.

Sycosis buys carnations
to mollify double chin.

B minor: sonata op. 35.
A pair of eyes roars out:
Don't splash the blood of Chopin around the place
for this crowd to slouch about in!
Hey, Gigi! Stop! –

The door dissolves: a woman.
Desert dried out. Canaanite brown.
Chaste. Full of caves. A scent comes with her. Hardly scent.
It's only a sweet leaning forward of the air
Against my brain.

A paunched obesity wobbles after her.[4]

By comparison with the examples from Hardy and Day Lewis, the points of view we occupy in this poem are cramped and repellent. Instead of looking down at a country from a great picturesque height we are brought up close to the pimples in a dissolute face. Consistently, Benn shoves the nose of the reader into a series of unpleasant places – one notices how there are no long views whatsoever in the poem, how we can in effect see no further than the repellent surfaces of the café, which creates an appropriately claustrophobic air. The effect of all this is strengthened by the consistent way in which Benn refers to people in terms of their attributes – the musicians are described in terms of their disabilities or diseases. This technique is itself a kind of close-up, zooming in on one quality of an individual at the expense of all others.

Many of the most satisfying effects result from combining constricting close-ups with expansive long shots. We can see a good example of this in 'Treatment', a prose-poem by C. D. Wright:

This is a 16-mm film of seven minutes in which no words are spoken. But for a few hand-tinted elements – the girl's dress, the sax, sky at church – the color is black-and-white. The camera reports in the all-knowing third except in hand-held shots when it momentarily exposes the driver's field of vision.

The bus rocks out of ruts and over creek rocks at predawn. The driver hasn't picked up any children. He has the radio on and a cigarette lit. Isn't paying attention to either. His headlights scan the road, and webs in the trees, as if they were searchlights. His mind is bent, as his posture and his face reveal. A girl dresses in purple in the dark. She feels along the wallpaper to the kitchen, fixes oatmeal, warms coffee to which she adds globs of honey. She makes a sandwich for lunch. She starts to eat out of the pot on the stove. Stops and gets a bowl from a high cabinet and sits at the table. She taps with her foot to a tune she hums only inside herself. When she goes back upstairs to comb her hair and make an irregular part, to tinkle – she hears her parents. Their bedsprings. A shot of them under many covers. Apparently her mother has told her she is a love child. She understands, so her listening isn't upsetting. She steals in her younger brother's room and leaves a bird she has folded from one sheet of paper on the nightstand. When she hears the bus shifting at the foot of the hill she grabs sweater and tablet and flies past the lunchsack on the banister. Their house isn't beautiful but its shadows are. The driver greets her with Hey Princess. That look. She sits close to the rear. The driver climbs the hill and puts it in neutral under an elm stand. He jerks the handbrake. The camera is in back and shooting forward as he comes down the aisle – it is behind her. He looms larger than he is and walks as if the bus were in motion. The rape is explicit. The camera shoots out the back and side windows every few seconds to see if anyone, another vehicle, approaches. There are no more shots of the girl. The parents' house is shown from the yard and from the foot of her window. Light breaks in the trees, a cool sun. You hear the bus grind, the children, as the bus fills and proceeds. Then a field of high grass, a white church. No roads leading there. No cars parked nearby. Slight quality of a different world. A saxophone is played. A full choir accompanies. A silent congregation: all stand, motionless. All adults. Pharoah Sanders stands in front of the choir stall in white robes. He plays with his eyes shut. He plays a curved soprano. His foot taps to an interior beat. Clearly he's an Angel. With the horn he lures. Accuses. His solo has a timeless aura. The doors of the church blow open. The driver falls onto the aisle. He begins to squirm on his belly toward the Pharoah. It is a long journey. The Pharoah wails controllably. The choir sways, claps; the congregation keeps quiet, light breaks in the trees and indistinct voices of many children fill the nave as if they were boarding a bus.[5]

C. D. Wright's prose-poem (I call it this for want of a better term; part of the effect of the piece is caused by our not knowing quite what it is) is a very contemporary example of how our viewpoints have been educated by visual media, particularly cinema and television. In the italicized directions at the beginning we are told that no words are spoken, a double-sided remark considering that all we have here are words. Furthermore, we are dealing with subject-matter, the rape of a child, for which, in one sense, no words are possible. The directions explicitly describe two kinds of viewpoint which are associated with recognizable kinds of cinematic shot, the objective 'all-knowing third[-person]' viewpoint and the subjective hand-held viewpoint of the driver. Clearly, there is a deliberate separation of these two points of view which is associated with a form of judgement. For most of the poem, we occupy the godlike objective position while the driver, whose viewpoint is shaky (a probable reflection of his mental state), offers us a viewpoint which we are reluctant to share. Even as we occupy this repellent position, however briefly, we are invited to feel something like guilt or horror, in much the same way as when we occupy the girl's position we feel fear or helplessness. These emotions are quite different from what we might feel if we were only given the bald facts of the case, if we were told, for example, that 30,000 people had died in a distant earthquake. On its own, this sort of statement is too remote for us to feel anything sharp. But in this prose-poem, we are invited to occupy two positions: the one who suffers and the one who inflicts suffering. Our reactions are correspondingly more intense.

This poem doesn't give us instructions as to how to react, and part of its power is in not letting us respond to material in a dead, rehearsed fashion. We are thrown back on our own resources. How should we respond to this 'treatment' of a 'film-script' which is not exactly a treatment or a film-script? How should we respond to this poem which is not quite a poem? The title gives us no answers but it is worth reflecting a little on its ambiguity. Wright uses a term which is taken from film culture (a 'treatment' is a short version of a film-script), but the word 'treatment' resonates in other ways. We encounter the sadistic treatment of a young girl as well as an unusual treatment of poetic form.

Your assignment is to write a poem which encompasses a number of widely differing viewpoints. Just some examples: (to maintain the cinematic metaphor) wide-angle shots, close-ups, shots of landscapes, of faces, shots from inside a coffee-cup, shots from the edge of the Milky Way, a sequence of rapidly changing shots, 'long exposure' shots and shots in slow motion.

Notes

1 James Gibson, ed., *The Variorum Edition of the Complete Poems of Thomas Hardy* (London: Macmillan, 1979), pp. 319–20.

2 Edward Mendleson, ed., *The English Auden: Poems, Essays and Dramatic Writings 1927–1939* (London: Faber, 1977), p. 141.

3 Robin Skelton, ed., *Poetry of the Thirties* (London: Penguin, 1964), pp. 49–50.

4 Trans. Michael Hamburger, in E. B. Ashton, ed., *Primal Vision: Selected Writings of Gottfried Benn* (New York: New Directions, 1960), p. 219.

5 C. D. Wright, *Steal Away: Selected and New Poems* (Port Townsend: Copper Canyon Press, 2002), pp. 42–3.

3

The Question of Voices

In this chapter we will be looking at what can happen when a poem contains more than one voice. The technical term for this device is polyphony. It should be apparent from my introduction that I regard polyphony as a good strategy, a way of getting around default ideas of what the poem is. It also helps to distance the writer from potentially disabling ideas of the poem as essentially a form of self-expression. We need not think of the poem as a bath-tub to be filled with the water of our personality. A multi-voiced poem invites us to think of the poem as a provisional space through which presences other than ourselves may pass – and occasionally have their say. But, unfortunately, we *are* conditioned to feel that a poem is about self-expression, indeed that a poem is about as personal an art-form as can be imagined. If one thinks about the embarrassment which novice writers often feel about showing their own poems to others, a good deal of this discomfort can be explained as a fear of exposure, as though each poem were a window opening dangerously on their 'inner personality'. Indeed, this suggests that the popular view of a poem as the ultimate form of self-expression is inhibiting, and might better be dismantled.

While nineteenth-century Romantic treatments of the poem tend to emphasize a single 'inspired' lyric voice, older traditions (especially the popular ballad) think of the poem in terms of a collective voice. Ballads depend on the idea of a community with shared, transmissible values, a place where the different voices of the community reach a kind of equilibrium.

Including multiple voices may also allow the poem to draw on the resources of other genres, particularly drama and the novel. W. B. Yeats, for example, owed much of the development of his poetry to his experience with theatre, the Romantic lyric I-persona of his earlier work giving way to the tension of voices in conflict or discussion. Including more than one voice invites the reader to question where the heart of the poem lies and some of the best-known twentieth-century poets have made powerful use of polyphony. In John Berryman's *Dream Songs*, for example, the speaker, 'Henry', is often engaged in a dialogue with an invisible other. Many of the poems of Robert Frost include a large slice of dialogue and often they read like short stories. For Frost human presence is found above all in voice, not in theories, and it is found in the delicate, subtle variations of tone which we all recognize from lived experience.

Multi-voiced poems can make the reading experience excitingly un-stable, inviting the reader to wonder which of the poem's voices is most prominent, which voice has most weight, which is most to be trusted. Multi-voiced poems invite us to be alert to the way language is actually *spoken*, to the emphases, pauses and hesitations which *written* language often overlooks.

Let us look first at a poem by Thomas Hardy:

WHO'S IN THE NEXT ROOM

'Who's in the next room? – who?
   I seemed to see
Somebody in the dawning passing through,
   Unknown to me.'
'Nay: you saw nought. He passed invisibly.'

'Who's in the next room? – who?
   I seem to hear
Somebody muttering firm in a language new
   That chills the ear.'
'No: you catch not his tongue who has entered there.'

'Who's in the next room? – who?
   I seem to feel
His breath like a clammy draught, as if it drew
   From the Polar Wheel.'
'No: none who breathes at all does the door conceal.'

'Who's in the next room? – who?
   A figure wan

37

> With a message to one in there of something due?
>   Shall I know him anon?'
> 'Yea he; and he brought such; and you'll know him anon.'[1]

Hardy's poem builds up a sense of tension and suspense in the inter-change between the two speakers. The voices are deliberately distinct – indeed we can tell them apart so easily that Hardy is able to dispense with con-versational markers like 'he said' and 'she said'. While the first voice is anxious and uncertain, the second voice is calm and assured. There is no scene-setting by an omniscient third party, and no attempt to specify location beyond implying that we are in some kind of house. This gives to readers an opportunity to use their imaginations and to supply the appro-priate details.

The poem begins with a dramatic question, made more dramatic by the concluding repetition of 'who?' – without this repetition we might read the opening as much more casual in tone than it is intended to be. By the end of the poem, thanks to the clues which are dropped in the conversa-tion, we have a likely answer to the question: Death. At the same time, this is no mere puzzle-poem – our interest in it does not end when we have 'solved' the mystery of the person in the next room. After all, we are no nearer to knowing the identity of the two speakers, or to learning why one of them seems better informed than the other. Not only that, but there appears to be a further person who has neither a voice nor a name in the next room, to whom Death is paying a fatal visit. It may be that Hardy is inviting us to consider how news of our own death will be received by others. Perhaps like the first voice in the poem someone who hears of our passing will think first about their own mortality.

It is useful to see how the two voices convey as much by their respec-tive tones as they do by what they outwardly say. The first voice is more obviously emotional and sharply registers the fear and confusion which we feel when thinking about our end. But the second voice, which combines flat 'yes' and 'no' answers with very definite-sounding statements, reflects something of the finality, the uncontradictable nature, of Death. By strip-ping away all but the most rudimentary of environmental conditions in the poem – all we can gather is that there are two rooms – Hardy allows the voices to fix themselves more firmly in our minds while at the same time 'underscoring' the nakedness of the human condition. These charac-ters, the poem suggests, are 'only' voices and perhaps the same might be said for the rest of us. The focus on voice is moving – we do not think of either voice as belonging exclusively to Hardy. Instead the poem gives voice to a wide set of human concerns. It avoids introversion.

In both of these poems, there is no narrator, and it is instructive to see what can happen when one is present. In the poems of Robert Frost, like 'Home Burial' or 'A Servant to Servants', for example, we often find a number of characters who get long speaking parts. Indeed Frost is so fond of speech in verse that his characters will often speak when no one else is present, blurting something out in a forest or shouting across a lake. More often, though, he uses dialogue, as in this very dark example, 'Not to Keep':

NOT TO KEEP

They sent him back to her. The letter came
Saying . . . And she could have him. And before
She could be sure there was no hidden ill
Under the formal writing, he was there,
Living. They gave him back to her alive –
How else? They are not known to send the dead. –
And not disfigured visibly. His face?
His hands? She had to look, to look and ask,
'What is it, dear?' And she had given all
And still she had all – *they* had – they the lucky!
Wasn't she glad now? Everything seemed won,
And all the rest for them permissible ease.
She had to ask, 'What was it, dear?'
                                        'Enough,
Yet not enough. A bullet through and through,
High in the breast. Nothing but what good care
And medicine and rest, and you a week,
Can cure me of to go again.' The same
Grim giving to do over for them both.
She dared no more than ask him with her eyes
How was it with him for a second trial.
And with his eyes he asked her not to ask.
They had given him back to her, but not to keep.[2]

Any poem which uses speech is also able to make use of what is not said. In conversation, we can conceal as much as we reveal. Whatever we say is also a matter of what we might have said, what we almost said, what we would have liked to say had we but world enough and time. Some poets are keenly aware of the what-is-not-said quality of conversation and Frost is certainly one of these.

'Not to Keep' circles around what it is best not to say. Indeed it begins with a broken-off sentence which stops before anything is specified, as though to repeat that which the letter *did* say would be to arouse too much fear – or too much hope. Of the three voices which the poem contains – man, woman and narrator – it is the third which is the most complex, at times sarcastically distancing itself from what is described ('How else? They are not known to send the dead'), at times identifying so closely with the woman that it mimics her agitation ('His face? / His hands? She had to look, to look and ask'). This tonal ambivalence is echoed by the exchange between the husband and the wife. The woman's anxiety is met by the husband's exhausted, artificial calm, and the matter-of-fact quality of his voice is meant to reassure. It is also meant to close off inquiry, as we gather when the woman breaks off her line of questions. That there are more questions that could be asked is obvious, but the woman realizes that they are best held back, and so the poem leaves all parties, woman, man, narrator, reader, to orbit around what has only been implied.

When the narrator takes over the poem again for the final time, the poem ends with a kind of snap, as the sound of the plosive 'p' foreshadows what the husband's fate will be. It is a poem of tremendous helplessness. The narrator does not even bother explaining who the 'they' represents – the army? The government? And which army? Which government? By being so unspecific the 'they' comes to stand for all impersonal forces which drive people apart, forces about which the poem is ultimately speechless.

A similar example of what might have been said can be found in the later poems of W. B. Yeats. These sometimes come across as being like short verse-plays. 'Adam's Curse' is a good example:

> We sat together at one summer's end,
> That beautiful mild woman, your close friend,
> And you and I, and talked of poetry.
> I said, 'A line will take us hours maybe;
> Yet if it does not seem a moment's thought,
> Our stitching and unstitching has been naught.
> Better go down upon your marrow-bones
> And scrub a kitchen pavement, or break stones
> Like an old pauper, in all kinds of weather;
> For to articulate sweet sounds together
> Is to work harder than all these, and yet

Be thought an idler by the noisy set
Of bankers, schoolmasters, and clergymen
The martyrs call the world.'
                              And thereupon
That beautiful mild woman for whose sake
There's many a one shall find out all heartache
On finding that her voice is sweet and low
Replied, 'To be born woman is to know –
Although they do not talk of it at school –
That we must labour to be beautiful.'

I said, 'It's certain there is no fine thing
Since Adam's fall but needs much labouring.
There have been lovers who thought love should be
So much compounded of high courtesy
That they would sigh and quote with learned looks
Precedents out of beautiful old books;
Yet now it seems an idle trade enough.'

We sat grown quiet at the name of love;
We saw the last embers of daylight die,
And in the trembling blue-green of the sky
A moon, worn as if it had been a shell
Washed by time's waters as they rose and fell
About the stars and broke in days and years.

I had a thought for no one's but your ears:
That you were beautiful, and that I strove
To love you in the old high way of love;
That it had all seemed happy, and yet we'd grown
As weary-hearted as that hollow moon.[3]

One of the major differences between Yeats's early style and his late style was the way the latter had been influenced by his work for the theatre. This experience came to colour his poetry, with impressive results. Many of Yeats's later poems seem like scenes from a longer drama – the reader comes to feel that they are stumbling in on an action which has been going on before they arrived and which will be going on after they have left. There is a similarity between this effect and the kind of effect produced by powerful opening lines like, for example, Auden's 'From the very first coming down'. Lines of this sort are, as it were, open at both ends – they convey a sense of something which precedes them and something towards which they will go afterwards. It is this capacity for a poem, or a single line, to point beyond itself which is such a valuable quality and which gives the sense of the poem as touched by independent life.

In 'Adam's Curse', we see an example of one of these dramatic scenes. The poem contains three voices – Yeats in the present looking back, Yeats in the past, and the 'beautiful mild woman'. Interestingly, we do not hear from the woman whom Yeats is primarily addressing, although we very much feel her dramatic presence. For example, one feels that the long speech which Yeats-in-the-past makes is an attempt to impress the woman he loves. He is performing. The situation which comes into view, a conversation with a pronounced erotic undercurrent, throws a particular light on the words which Yeats is using. As much as what is being said – Yeats pontificating about the nature of poetry – we feel the pressure of what he does not say. The voice of the 'beautiful mild woman' contrasts with Yeats's in being more succinct and in putting the point about labour from a woman's perspective. Although there is no argument in the poem, there is yet a sense that the three people present are not in complete agreement. In particular we see the way the conversation moves in a particular direction, one that has been impelled by the emotional undercurrents between the characters. The conversation moves towards love, in other words, because it is in the minds of the characters, particularly Yeats. This is one way in which the dramatic situation allows the reader to feel something of what has gone before, even if that which has gone before is not spelt out in explicit detail. Because all of the characters know about the emotional undercurrents between themselves they naturally grow quiet 'at the name of love'. They are being careful because they do not want to open old wounds. We see the way Yeats handles this dramatic point by shifting from the voice of himself as a dramatic character to the voice of the narrator looking back. This shift of tone and time heavily underlines the key moment and prepares the way for the melancholy and reflective conclusion.

Often, the power of voice derives from irregular use of language, the freshness of idiomatic expression. Yeats's voices are relatively formal. By way of contrast, here is how a more colloquial poet, Charles Bukowski, uses voices in his poem 'my old man':

16 years old
during the depression
I'd come home drunk

and all my clothing –
shorts, shirts, stockings –
suitcase, and pages of
short stories
would be thrown out on the
front lawn and about the
street.

my mother would be waiting behind a tree:
'Henry, Henry, don't
go in . . . he'll
kill you, he's read
your stories . . .'

'I can whip his
ass . . .'

'Henry, please take
this . . . and
find yourself a room.'

but it worried him
that I might not
finish high school
so I'd be back
again.

one evening he walked in
with the pages of
one of my short stories
(which I had never submitted
to him)

and he said, 'this is
a great short story.'
I said, 'o.k.,'
and he handed it to me
and I read it.
it was a story about
a rich man
who had a fight with
his wife and had

gone out into the night
for a cup of coffee
and had observed
the waitress and the spoons
and the forks and the
salt and pepper shakers
and the neon signs
in the window
and then had gone back
to his stable
to see and touch his
favourite horse
who then
kicked him in the head
and killed him.

somehow
the story held
meaning for him
though
when I had written it
I had no idea
of what I was
writing about.

so I told him,
'o.k., old man, you can
have it.'
and he took it
and walked out
and closed the door.
I guess that's
as close
as we ever got.[4]

In contrast to the poem by Yeats, Bukowski gives us an inarticulate narrator. Yet there is value in this too. The voice in this poem is one the reader will probably not identify as the author's – this would seem to be the case because the narrator is noticeably inarticulate, like the kind of speaker we might find in a Raymond Carver story. The speaker will probably strike us as being far removed from the kind of voice we would normally consider 'poetic'. Indeed the speaker seems almost uncomfortable with the formal confines of a poem and not especially 'sorry' when the poem comes to an end. Looking through the poem we find too an absence of poetic devices – there are no metaphors or similes or images. It is in this sense a deliberately impoverished poem.

Nevertheless one of the things which the poem does contain is voices. We might say there are four of them: the father, the mother, the narrator in the present looking back and the narrator in the past. We might not usually stop to separate the latter two except that the narrator in his story-telling capacity is also thinking back to a time when he was younger – the storyteller is more articulate than his younger self. The narrator-in-the-present does most of the speaking to us, but the fact that we hear all four voices is significant. The mother is only very briefly heard – and we register the worry and concern in her voice – we have seen how well an anxious voice can work before in the poems by Hardy and Frost. Bukowski also wants to make use of the fact that the voices get to say so little. We learn from the narrator that the incident with the short story amounted to one of the most significant events in the speaker's life, the moment when he is closest to his father – yet what the voices say about that moment is almost comically minimal. The fact that we also hear nothing more about the mother is almost comically sad.

So what have the voices added to this poem? Mainly, presences. We sense much more through what they say than what is said about them or much more in the gap between what they say and what is said about them. Also, the way that the characters speak in the poem shows that despite their lack of eloquence there is between them a family feeling, even a family language. Their inability to express themselves is shared and they seem to recognize that this is so. The final element which links the poem together is the contrast between the blunt, abbreviated statements of the characters and the relatively long sentence which the narrator uses to recapitulate his short story. The narrator's voice is slightly ironic, slightly dismissive of the literariness of his own story – but it is even more ironic that this story (which as he admits he doesn't really understand himself) provides his one point of contact with the old man.

Your assignment is to write a poem containing more than one voice. You might try to include voices which are obviously in tension, or in competition, with each other. Try to use at least one voice which uses idiomatic language, and to give a sense of the way one voice influences the expression of another. It might also be useful to include a speaker who is not saying what they really want to say.

Notes

1 James Gibson, ed., *The Variorum Edition of the Complete Poems of Thomas Hardy* (London: Macmillan, 1979), pp. 503–4.
2 Edward Connery Latham, ed., *The Poetry of Robert Frost* (New York: Henry Holt, 1979), pp. 230–1.
3 W. B. Yeats, *Collected Poems*, 1st edn. 1933, 2nd edn. 1950 (London: Macmillan, 1982), pp. 89–90.
4 Charles Bukowski, *Love is a Dog from Hell: Poems 1974–1977*, 1st edn. 1977 (Santa Rosa: Black Sparrow Press, 1991), pp. 292–4.

4

The Question of Scale

Is the universe large? Is a fly small? In our everyday way of thinking, the answer to both questions is 'yes'. But a poem is not an everyday way of thinking. The relational view of poetry recommended in this book is well illustrated by the matter of size, for size, like everything else, is relative. A poem can surprise and delight us when it reminds us of this fact, when it sets a mosquito beside the Milky Way. Just as the relationship between the small and the large reflects the relationship between the poem and the world, so it underlies one of the most important poetic devices: metonymy, the relationship of part to whole. A poem is necessarily a partial experience of the world around us. So how does this finite part speak to the potentially infinite? One way is to write poetry which makes deliberate use of changes of scale, poetry which moves purposefully from the large to the small. Consider this delightful, self-consciously tiny, poem by Emily Dickinson:

> To make a prairie it takes a clover and one bee,
> One clover, and a bee,
> And revery.
> The revery alone will do,
> If bees are few.[1]

Just as some people are fond of living in modest flats, and some of living in fantastic mansions, so poets have a feeling for and against objects, spaces and creatures built on different scales. Randall Jarrell might have had Emily Dickinson in mind when he said that all cultivated American poets are afraid of size. Certainly, as she raises up some tiny things, Dickinson seems to put the prairie down. But there is another point.

Dickinson suggests that to call to mind something as large as a prairie all we need are a few small points of reference. We might put it like this: at any time we can refer to 'a universe' but that reference will not come alive if it is not focused on specific things. We need our imagining of that universe to be anchored in something specific – an octopus, say, or a cactus. When we imagine the large, we need to trace a relationship from the small – and vice versa. So Dickinson's prairie starts with a bee. There may be many bees and much clover in any prairie, but if we cannot bring single examples of this sort to mind then the prairie will not be alive for us.

In his 'Auguries of Innocence', William Blake makes use of the same kind of principle. Here is the beginning of the poem:

> To see a World in a Grain of Sand,
> And a Heaven in a Wild Flower,
> Hold Infinity in the palm of your hand,
> And Eternity in an hour.
>
> A Robin Red breast in a Cage
> Puts all Heaven in a Rage.
> A dove-house fill'd with doves and Pigeons
> Shudders hell thro' all its regions.
> A dog starved at his Master's Gate
> Predicts the ruin of the State.
> A horse misus'd upon the Road
> Calls to Heaven for Human blood.[2]

Indeed, poems can bring the whole concept of size into question. What does it mean to describe things as 'small' or 'large', as 'finite' or 'infinite'? Does our 'language of size' (to borrow Auden's phrase) usefully reflect our experience of the world? A poem reminds us how much our habit of sizing falls between us and what we see. Hence Blake begins his 'Auguries of Innocence' with just such a thought: 'To *see* a World in a Grain of Sand' (my emphasis) – Blake understands that there is a choice. A poem can choose to enlarge or diminish, and that very choice becomes part of the drama of our reading.

In the midst of events which are beyond normal comprehension, small details can cut little keyholes of understanding. Apollinaire's 'The Little Car' deals with just such an event: the outbreak of World War I. Against an intensely imagined backdrop, the poem moves from the solemnly major ('Unimaginable heights') to the comically minor ('a burst tyre'). The whole poem is a conflict between objects and ideas which are constructed on radically different scales. The small details, to which Apollinaire pays warm attention, humanize the larger tragedy:

THE LITTLE CAR

On August 31 1914
I left Deauville shortly before midnight
In Rouveyre's little car

Counting the chauffeur there were three of us

We said farewell to a whole era
Furious giants were looming over Europe
Eagles left their eyries to wait for the sun
Voracious fish rose up from the depths
Whole nations were eager to know one another more deeply
And were rushing towards one another
The dead trembled with fear in their dark dwellings

The dogs were all barking at the frontiers
And I carried inside me all these armies that were fighting
I felt them rise up inside me I felt whole countries spread out as the
    armies wound through them
Belgium's forests and happy villages
Francorchamps Eau Rouge and its springs
Always a favoured region for invasions
Railway arteries along which men on their way to die
Gave one last salute to life and its colours
Deep oceans where monsters were stirring
In old shipwrecked carcasses
Unimaginable heights where men fight
Higher than eagles soar
Man fights there against man
And falls suddenly like a shooting star

Within me I felt skilful new beings
Building and arranging a new universe
A merchant of unheard-of wealth and prodigious stature
Was laying out an extraordinary display of wares
And huge shepherds led

Great silent flocks that grazed on words
And were barked at by all the dogs on the road

I shall never forget that night journey during which none of us said a word
O dark departure with our three headlights dying
O tender night from before the war
O villages towards which blacksmiths summoned between midnight and
  one in the morning were hurriedly making their way
Not far from Lisieux the very blue or Versailles the golden
And we had to stop three times to change a burst tyre

And when after passing through Fontainebleau
In the afternoon
We arrived in Paris
Just as the mobilization was being posted
My friend and I both understood
That the little car had driven us into a
New Era
And that although we were both mature men
We had only just been born[3]

How to deal with such a world-changing event? Apollinaire offers the surprising intimacy of a car journey, although it turns out that the poem is as much one of transformation as of transportation. The changes which are going on within the speaker and his friend are at least as important as the changes taking place outside them.

One of the most striking features of the poem is the way that it parcels out information. If we take away the first line, for example, we would have an opening substantially different in tone: a brisk transmission of the speaker's position, like the beginning of a detective story. With the first line in place, however, we look set to meet a different kind of experience – perhaps the speaker is remembering his first love, or the moment when he heard about the death of a parent? And why are we told that the car belongs to Rouveyre when we hear little further about the speaker's friend? We might wonder why he does not use the phrase, 'my friend's little car'. The beginning of the poem continues to dispense information of no obvious significance. This is especially true of line 4, which comes after a pause that might indicate a substantial change of poetic direction. The reader might feel *well, the scene-setting is over – now the author will introduce his main line of thought.* Instead the speaker counts the number of people in the car and indicates that someone else, about whom we will hear nothing further, is driving. What has been achieved, though, is evident. The impression of a fragile, little world has been created, which lingers through the poem even as we encounter a set of sinister images built on a gigantic scale.

The poem continues to puzzle us with minor details. Why are we told that the characters stop three times to change a burst tyre? When we look closer we see that there are some understated links between these apparently unconnected details. For example, there are three people in the car, the car has three headlights and it stops three times. It seems important that the speaker is not travelling on his own, just as it is important that the design of this little community is matched by the design of another little community, the car itself. One small construction reflects on the other. This matching of designs, three heads and three headlights, is of a piece with the other implied connections. Objects in the poem realize themselves, sometimes very negatively, within each other. At the most intense point of the whole poem, for instance, the speaker describes a universe of death being constructed inside himself.

We might ponder the title – it is after all called 'The *Little* Car'. Apollinaire makes quiet equations between the little car, the little communities and indeed the little poem itself, but the poet does nothing to sentimentalize this equation. It is not a question of merely opposing littleness (good) to bigness (bad). Rather, Apollinaire is showing how the small is implicated in the large. We sense this not only in his self-description but also in some of his unusual formulae for describing the conflict: 'Whole nations were eager to know one another more deeply'. There is irony in this, of course, but it chimes too with the poem's uneasy attitude to the technological – from those modern 'railway arteries' which will transport multitudes to their death to the little car itself which after all may only be a ghostly cog in the machine.

In his poem 'Model toward a Theory of Cognition', Hans Magnus Enzensberger invites us to think about the relational nature of size. Nothing, after all, is *truly* large or truly small, since objects can only be relatively small or large when they are placed next to something else, or when they are assessed according to some conventional standard of measurement:

MODEL TOWARD A THEORY OF COGNITION

Here is a box for you,
a large box

51

labelled
Box.
Open it,
and you will find
a box in it,
labelled
Box from a box
labelled Box.
Look into it
(I mean this box now,
not the other one),
and you will find a box
labelled
And so on,
and if you go on
like this,
you will find,
after infinite efforts,
an infinitely small
box
with a label
so tiny
that the lettering,
as it were,
dissolves
before your eyes.
It is a box
existing only
in your imagination.
A perfectly empty
box.[4]

Enzensberger's poem also encourages us to dwell on a progressive sequence of relationships, since the poem depends upon imagining an object which gets ever smaller. Such a diminishing series can be very satisfying for the reader to contemplate, since it presupposes a kind of logical order – it structures the imaginative efforts of the reader in a way that is easy to grasp. Enzensberger uses this device in part to ironic effect. On the one hand, the perfectly empty box of the conclusion may refer to what the imagination has produced; on the other, it may refer to the imagination itself. Enzensberger also shows the value of a minimum of means – the poem has all the bareness of a cartoon — no carnival of objects on display here — and yet it has a long-lasting fascination and can be read with delight over and over.

In Gottfried Benn's 'Little Aster' we find the poet making a deliberately lurid use of metonymy. As in Apollinaire's poem, our attention is drawn to scale by the title, although in this case Benn intends something sarcastic, a kind of fraudulent sweetness:

LITTLE ASTER

A drowned truck-driver was propped on the slab.
Someone had stuck a lavender aster
between his teeth.
As I cut out the tongue and the palate,
through the chest
under the skin,
with a long knife,
I must have touched the flower, for it slid
into the brain lying next.
I packed it into the cavity of the chest
among the excelsior
as it was sewn up.
Drink yourself full in your vase!
Rest softly,
little aster![5]

If all we knew about the poem was its title — and we did not know anything about the author — we might expect something rather gooey, a pretty little poem about a pretty little flower. Small, after all, is 'beautiful'. The poem plays against this rather obvious expectation, while going a little way — but only a little way — to meet it. For example, the concluding lines provide us with exactly the kind of sentimental statement the title might lead us to expect. But by this stage, the graphic details of the corpse persuade us that we are in quite a different sort of poem. We might wonder what Benn is trying to achieve — is he being deliberately disgusting by placing the slice of brain next to the little flower? The poem seems to want us to register disgust, not with the truck-driver, but with how the truck-driver is seen. The poem is trying to shock us into a disturbing perspective — in the presence of a sentimental flower to make us look through very unsentimental eyes. Benn's minimalism shows us the power of arranging a smaller object such that we guess about a larger whole.

Human beings always try to make strange situations familiar, try to incorporate new stimuli into their existing picture of the world – indeed this is what it is to make sense, to make new knowledge line up with old. But our minds can only change a little at a time, not all at once. To digest the new we need to chew on it one small chunk at a time. The image of a little aster is something which our minds can easily consume. At the same time, the rest of the poem provides us with various suggestions for how to work on that image. Although it avoids definite conclusions, it offers us a range of directional cues. With only a few small juxtapositions, Benn's poem provokes us into more wide-ranging speculation.

For our final example, here is a popular and attractive poem from the work of Robert Browning:

MEETING AT NIGHT

1

The grey sea and the long black land;
And the yellow half-moon large and low;
And the startled little waves that leap
In fiery ringlets from their sleep,
As I gain the cove with pushing prow,
And quench its speed i' the slushy sand.

2

Then a mile of warm sea-scented beach;
Three fields to cross till a farm appears;
A tap at the pane, the quick sharp scratch
And blue spurt of a lighted match,
And a voice less loud, through its joys and fears,
Than the two hearts beating each to each![6]

Browning is a poet who likes to leave a lot of material out. Like many of his poems, 'Meeting at Night' depends a good deal on suggestion and implication. Simply to draw attention to many of the questions which the poem raises, but does not answer – and which we might reasonably expect it to answer – is revealing: who is the speaker? Where are they exactly? Who are they meeting? What kind of relationship is it? And why are they meeting in this seemingly clandestine fashion? While we may *expect* these questions to be answered, we may not *want* to hear the answers. For this is a poem which owes its considerable popularity to how much and how easily the reader can project themselves into the scene.

The poem is also popular because of its clever use of scale. It begins with a distant, generalized description, phrased in such a way as to suggest that the speaker can see a wide expanse of land and sea (in other words, the speaker is not lying face down on the ground or caught-up in a thicket), and it ends inside two people – and where their hearts are beating, of course, nothing can be seen. The first line is deliberately nondescript, in part so that the large space it evokes will contrast all the more sharply with the tiny flare and the tight intimacy of the conclusion. The movement in the poem from large to small is purposeful and direct – like Enzenberger's poem, it represents a diminishing series and nothing is allowed to stand in the speaker's way. It is worth pointing out that it represents the kind of movement we undertake routinely in our lives. The movement towards and away from home (or a place that we feel at home in) is usually a movement through large spaces we do not know well to small spaces we know in fine detail – indeed we move through the former *for the sake of* the latter. This simple trajectory, so routine that we barely think about it, is one the poem follows, and which it intensifies with a rapid change of scale.

Your assignment is to write a poem which makes vigorous use of changes of scale. You might try to order these changes in a deliberate way. For example, you might begin the poem with a large object and end with a small one. Or you might have many small objects in the poem and only one large one. Try to let the changes of scale work significantly on whatever it is you want the poem to evoke.

Notes

1 Thomas H. Johnson, ed., *The Complete Poems of Emily Dickinson* (Boston: Little, Brown, 1960), p. 710.
2 Peter Butter, ed., *William Blake: Selected Poems* (London: Everyman, 1996), p. 77.
3 Robert Chandler, ed., *Apollinaire* (London: Everyman, 2000).
4 Hans Magnus Enzensberger, *Selected Poems*, trans. Hans Magnus Enzensberger and Michael Hamburger (Newcastle: Bloodaxe, 1994).
5 Trans. Babette Deutsch, in E. B. Ashton, ed., *Primal Vision: Selected Writings of Gottfried Benn* (New York: New Directions, 1960), p. 213.
6 M. H. Abrams, ed., *The Norton Anthology of English Literature. Vol. 2*, 4th edn. (New York: Norton, 1979).

5

Uses of Repetition

To repeat something is the simplest form of music, the simplest way to secure attention. It is fundamental to how we think: we learn by repetition; language itself probably arose from it. Consider what happens when you listen, for the first time, to an unfamiliar language. Any repetitions in the structure will immediately stand out, because your mind is already looking for them. It is the first thing which code-breakers seek in a message they want to decrypt. When speaking to a very young child, we repeat sounds emphatically because we know that the child is receptive to simple repeated patterns, hence the structure of children's nursery rhymes. The mind tries to familiarize the unfamiliar, and what it first seeks are points of repetition. It is hardly surprising that, used deliberately and carefully, repetition is a source of powerful literary effects.

As a literary tool, repetition is under-employed. Sometimes we may associate having to repeat ourselves with talking to someone who is not paying attention, or who is not very intelligent. Because of that, writers may feel that repetition is a little childish, and look for more obviously sophisticated devices. But there is no need to shy away from repetition – it may have primitive origins but it can be used in powerful and subtle ways. In poetry, repetition creates a sense of expectation (and therefore tension when that expectation is not, for a while, immediately satisfied). As the poems in this chapter illustrate, many effects are possible: hypnotic; insistent; oracular; tense.

Because it is as old as culture, new forms of repetition are likely to echo ancient ones. Many of the parallelistic structures in the poetry of William Blake and Walt Whitman, for example, deliberately echo the poetry of the Old Testament, and it is these structures which help those poets to convey a sense of prophetic authority. In dramatic speech, and in the speeches of politicians, repetition is an especially powerful tool. It can be used to sway a crowd, to move a group of people in a single emotional direction. In our first example, Mark Antony's famous speech from Shakespeare's play *Julius Caesar*, we see repetitive language being used to work a gathering of Roman citizens. Note how the repeated words and phrases become increasingly ironic (a repeated phrase may not always have the same meaning second time around). The lines are from act 3, scene 2, lines 73–107:

Friends, Romans, countrymen, lend me your ears;
I come to bury Caesar, not to praise him.
The evil that men do lives after them;
The good is oft interred with their bones;
So let it be with Caesar. The noble Brutus
Hath told you Caesar was ambitious;
If it were so, it was a grievous fault,
And grievously hath Caesar answer'd it.
Here, under leave of Brutus and the rest,
(For Brutus is an honourable man;
So are they all, all honourable men)
Come I to speak in Caesar's funeral.
He was my friend, faithful and just to me:
But Brutus says he was ambitious;
And Brutus is an honourable man.
He hath brought many captives home to Rome,
Whose ransoms did the general coffers fill.
Did this in Caesar seem ambitious?
When that the poor have cried, Caesar hath wept;
Ambition should be made of sterner stuff;
Yet Brutus says he was ambitious;
And Brutus is an honourable man.
You all did see that on the Lupercal
I thrice presented him a kingly crown,
Which he did thrice refuse: was this ambition?
Yet Brutus says he was ambitious;
And, sure, he is an honourable man.
I speak not to disprove what Brutus spoke,
But here I am to speak what I do know.
You all did love him once, not without cause:
What cause withholds you then to mourn for him?
O judgement! thou art fled to brutish beasts,

> And men have lost their reason. Bear with me;
> My heart is in the coffin there with Caesar,
> And I must pause till it come back to me.[1]

In general, dramatic speeches illustrate the value of capturing an imagined moment, a particular state of affairs to which the speaker is responding. Mark Antony's speech is, of course, intended to operate in a specific theatrical context – when it is taken out of that context we need to provide a supporting explanation for what is going on. Happily, the situation of the above speech is, like the play from which it is taken, well known. Mark Antony is reacting to the plotters who have disposed of Caesar, and of these Brutus is the most prominent. Mark Antony is employing his rhetorical skills, and a barrage of rhetorical devices, in order to achieve a specific effect: to turn the Roman crowd against the plotters. Therefore he must project his speech, as though through a loud-hailer, to incite the passions of the crowd. It is not a moment for careful, complicated arguments on his part. There are many repetitions within the speech – repeated words and repeated phrases. Antony uses these to set up a contrast between Caesar (repeated eight times) and Brutus (repeated nine times). Obviously a lot of the force of the contrast would be lost were Antony to name all the conspirators against Caesar. A swifter form of verbal action is needed. By naming Brutus, he in effect names all the conspirators against Caesar.

As the speech begins we think that Antony is going to speak only about Caesar. Our first inkling – at this point it is no more – that the speech may have an unexpected purpose is created by the early aside when he refers to the 'noble' Brutus. As the speech progresses the word 'Brutus' keeps returning with unusual persistence, as though the speaker kept coming back to some thought which he cannot quite form. Since the phrase 'Brutus is an honourable man' is quite banal in itself, as listeners we are persuaded that there must be something beyond the surface meaning which the speaker wants to gesture towards. Given that the phrase is not sonically impressive, there must be, so the mind thinks, another reason for Antony to repeat it.

Antony reinforces this sense of doubt and unease in the listener's mind by casting doubt on one of the key claims which Brutus makes against Caesar, that he was an ambitious man. While apparently reassuring the crowd about the intentions of Brutus, Mark Antony undermines this charge with vivid, highly emotional examples of Caesar's work for his people. By contrast with these colourful examples which tend to put Caesar in a good light, the repeated reference to the nobility of Brutus is colourless and tends to put *him* in a bad light. This speech clearly demonstrates that words always carry more than their dictionary meanings. Especially in performance, words can come to mean their opposites.

While Mark Antony's speech shows how powerful an instrument repetition can be as a means of swaying an emotional crowd, the technique can also be used for much gentler purposes. In Christopher Smart's portrait of his cat, we see it used affectionately. Smart was a devotional poet, so this is more than a poem merely about his speaker's pet. Smart wants to show how the workings of the divine can be traced in the movements of his pet. The way in which he goes about this has a simple charm. Here is an excerpt:

> For I will consider my Cat Jeoffry.
> For he is the servant of the Living God, duly and daily serving him.
> For at the first glance of the glory of God in the East he worships in his way.
> For is this done by wreathing his body seven times around with elegant
> quickness.
> For then he leaps up to catch the musk, which is the blessing of God
> upon his prayer.
> For he rolls upon prank to work it in.
> For having done duty and received blessing he begins to consider himself.
> For this he performs in ten degrees.
> For first he looks upon his fore-paws to see if they are clean.
> For secondly he kicks up behind to clear away there.
> For thirdly he works it upon stretch with the fore-paws extended.
> For fourthly he sharpens his paws by wood.
> For fifthly he washes himself.
> For sixthly he rolls upon wash.
> For Seventhly he fleas himself, that he may not be interrupted upon the beat.
> For Eighthly he rubs himself against a post.
> For Ninthly he looks up for his instructions.
> For Tenthly he goes in quest of food.
> For having consider'd God and himself he will consider his neighbour.
> For if he meets another cat he will kiss her in kindness.
> For when he takes his prey he plays with it to give it a chance.
> For one mouse in seven escapes by his dallying.[2]

The use of phrases which have a similar structure is known as parallelism. As a technique, it is often favoured by poets who want to compile catalogues, to pile one detail on top of another. However, if one uses this technique it is wise to ensure that one has a sufficiently interesting set of details to compile. Smart's record of the gestures of his cat is so minutely observed that that we do not get bored by his persistent listing, or by the emphatic repetitions which do so much to command our attention. Not only are these details of feline behaviour well realized, they are also linked together in a very logical way. The 'ten degrees' of the cat's daily ritual are a good example of this. They are also a good example of relationality working to the advantage of the poem. The actions of the cat are recreated as a whole, with one action flowing logically into another. All of the lines are therefore working on each other, and helping to define each other. The poet is able to tell us, for example, that the cat allows one mouse in seven to escape, because the cat's behaviour is itself repetitive, and has been repeatedly observed by his master. By implication, the actions of the cat are repeatedly observed, too, by his divine master. So the structure of the poem moulds itself to the order of this harmonious, habitual relationship.

Here is a poem by Miroslav Holub, which, in contrast to Smart's, uses repetition in an understated manner:

BRIEF REFLECTION ON ACCURACY

Fish
    always accurately know where to move and when,
    and likewise
    birds have an accurate built-in time sense
    and orientation.

Humanity, however,
    lacking such instincts resorts to scientific
    research. Its nature is illustrated by the following
    occurrence.

A certain soldier
    had to fire a cannon at six o'clock sharp every evening.
    Being a soldier he did so. When his accuracy was
    investigated he explained:

I go by
    the absolutely accurate chronometer in the window
    of the clockmaker down in the city. Every day at seventeen
    forty-five I set my watch by it and

climb the hill where my cannon stands ready.
At seventeen fifty-nine precisely I step up to the cannon
and at eighteen hours sharp I fire.

And it was clear
that this method of firing was absolutely accurate.
All that was left was to check that chronometer. So
the clockmaker down in the city was questioned about
his instrument's accuracy.

Oh, said the clockmaker,
This is one of the most accurate instruments ever. Just imagine,
For many years now a cannon has been fired at six o'clock sharp.
And every day I look at this chronometer
And always it shows exactly six.

So much for accuracy.
And fish move in the water, and from the skies
comes a rushing of wings while

Chronometers tick and cannon boom.[3]

Holub's poem is effectively an argument in verse, carefully reinforced by
the discreet use of repeated words and sentence-patterns. The word which
is repeated most often is 'accuracy', but as other examples in this chapter
show, repeated words do not always signify the same thing every time they
appear. Indeed the repetition of 'accuracy' here serves a purpose similar to
that of Mark Antony's repetition of 'ambitious'. When we first encounter
the word 'accuracy', we will not be inclined to question the concepts for
which it usually stands. Accuracy in human affairs, and scientific accuracy
in particular, we usually see as a matter of fact. Either a statement or a measurement is accurate or it is not. But Holub wants to challenge this pre-
sumption. His little parable is intended to suggest that accuracy in human
affairs is more a matter of getting our statements and measurements *to line
up with each other* than it is a matter of getting them to line up with the
'true state' of the world. His chosen example is time. The measurement of
time is itself bound up with repetition, with repeated intervals which take
their cue from the earth's relationship to the sun. Hence the 'six o'clock'
which is a measurement on which we rely throughout our lives, and so
the poem also repeats the phrase – and repeats, too, a pattern of words

indicative of accuracy: how ready we are to be persuaded that an 'exact' measurement is absolutely exact because it has been described as such. Precision is part of the rhetoric of specialists (like soldiers and clock-makers) which non-specialists are inclined to accept at face value. Holub's example reminds us that 'accuracy' is a relative term. One way Holub amplifies his theme, and keeps the issue of relationality before us, is how he repeats a pattern of pairs. When we measure we set one thing against another. The poem does something similar when it makes a pair of fish *and* birds, and another pair of soldier *and* clockmaker. The fish and birds, representing the power of forces beyond humanity, return at the end of the poem as a way of indicating the limits of our human concepts like 'accuracy'. This dry and sceptical poem contains few flashy phrases, but it represents the power of a well-written poem to make us question our view of the world.

Here is an example of my own use of repetition, in a poem which contains a number of sentences which begin with the word 'perhaps':

PERHAPS THEN

Perhaps the sun now shudders and goes down
one island further along.
Perhaps the sea remembers its shawl
one inch higher up the sea-wall.
Perhaps the big spheres in the early grasses,
the beads of sweat on gravestone faces

drop fractionally faster to Earth.
Perhaps no one goes in to Seán's bar any more.
Perhaps Mac has had it up to here

with abalones, with the TV thumping,
with a brother who can't hear his own swallow.
Perhaps the band in O'Rourke's has learnt how to play.

Perhaps Máirtín has scoured all the scurf off his boat
and Cha, in ramming it, ramming it home,
no longer gives out, 'it's a goooal'.
Perhaps Dundass has taken his sun by the throat.

Perhaps Taig is no longer quite Taigeen
and his parents no longer mention heaven

and where the rusty gate hangs on to its indecision
perhaps Lemass has compressed his whole fortune

into an Eden of crag and nettle.
Perhaps the world no longer stops at Jack's gate
and strolls out of town by a different route
and the ass has stepped from its long-standing mound
and the trees by the stream make a lazier sound.

Perhaps the houses at night flicker
                  rather than shine
and the car-lights move in an unbroken line.

Or where window sweeps and car skids in
where shore gleams and shirt buttons down
where dog spills, cloud cools and pub steams
where pier clicks, boat leans, wheel buckles and wire hums,
perhaps nothing at all has changed.

Perhaps then you will stay.[4]

One of my concerns in this poem was to use the repetitions as a way of anchoring the movement of the thought, allowing a wide variety of dreams and speculations to play against the pulse of the repeated word. The poem is a kind of question. It dramatizes a mind thinking through alternative possibilities, testing one against another, nervously seeking some image or memory which will explain its own agitation. As in the speech from *Julius Caesar*, the repetitions here indicate an urgent matter, something from which the speaker's mind is unable to turn away. As in those other examples, this refusal to turn away encourages the reader to 'look through' the words of the speaker to the imagined source of the unhappiness.

Of the other examples in this chapter, the structure of 'Perhaps Then' most resembles that of Christopher Smart's poem (though there is of course a noticeable difference in mood). Phrases are repeated at the head of a large number of the sentences in a poem of irregular line-length. Smart's poem and my own use the varying length of the lines to convey a sense of different speeds. Where the speaker of my poem's thought is excited and agitated, the poem 'speeds up', the repetitions become more insistent and regular. Where the speaker seems to be less confident, for example, ten lines from the end, the rhythm becomes more halting, departs from the built-up pattern, and seems to lose its way. At the conclusion of the poem, where the speaker seems at last to have hit on a thought which he wants very much to get across, the poem moves at its fastest speed. The speaker has foreseen his conclusion, knows where the poem is going to go and moves there briskly.

Your assignment is to write a poem making extensive use of repetition. I have in mind some fairly obvious parallelistic structures. For example, you might have every sentence or line beginning with the word 'And . . .', or with the phrase 'As though . . .'. Or you might decide to repeat a striking individual word like 'mojo' or 'omphalos'. The repetitions need not come in every line, but they should appear several times. Overall, I would like you to use repetition to create a sense of energy and excitement.

Notes

1   Michael Macmillan, ed., *The Works of Shakespeare: The Tragedy of Julius Caesar*, 1st edn. 1902 (London: Macmillan, 1917), pp. 105–6.
2   N. Callan, ed., *The Collected Poems of Christopher Smart Vol. 1* (London: Routledge, 1949), pp. 311–12.
3   Miroslav Holub, *On the Contrary and Other Poems*, trans. Ewald Osers (Newcastle: Bloodaxe, 1984), p. 16.
4   John Redmond, *Thumb's Width* (Manchester: Carcanet, 2001).

6

Image

Given that we live in a media culture which forces us to be visually literate, it is sensible to think about the status of the image in poetry. In the history of twentieth-century poetry, it is difficult to separate that status from the influence of the movement known as Imagism. As a set of principles and practices developed by poets like T. E. Hulme and Ezra Pound, Imagism sought to replace the vagueness and sentimentality of the period's poetry with a new hardness and exactitude. Imagism held that visual perceptions were prior to, and therefore of a quality greater than, language. Classic Imagist poems tend to present images with a minimum of narrative detail or commentary and are often highly impersonal. Hulme's poems themselves are very short (and very few) and usually leave the mind with an exact, but highly suggestive, image that is not susceptible to simple paraphrase or interpretation. As Hulme put it: 'Images in verse are not mere decoration, but the very essence of an intuitive language.' For Hulme, description truly was revelation enough.

Strict Imagism did not endure, but the movement's influence – its emphasis on the precise, the concrete, the unsentimental, on images sufficiently powerful to speak for themselves – is still felt. It is difficult to detach that influence from developments in the visual arts, in particular the movement away from narrative in modern painting. Other currents of thought, like Surrealism, made an impression. Illustrating the principles of the Surrealist movement, David Gascoyne's poem in this chapter runs together improbable images without overt commentary. Influenced by the teachings of Sigmund Freud, such poems seek to explore the image-making power of the subconscious.

Because of their emphasis on a single striking visual perception, images in modern poetry often have a static, photographic quality. Such stillness can be a major part of the poem's effect, as it picks out for emphasis a particular moment, a particular scene frozen in the poem's viewfinder. Of course, imagery can also convey a sense of flux. As we will see in Jorie Graham's poem, 'Notes on the Reality of the Self', a sequence of images carefully juxtaposed may create an energetic sense of movement.

To begin, here is a poem called 'Autumn' by T. E. Hulme:

> A touch of cold in the Autumn night
> I walked abroad,
> And saw the ruddy moon lean over a hedge
> Like a red-faced farmer.
> I did not stop to speak, but nodded;
> And round about were the wistful stars
> With white faces like town children.[1]

At first sight, we may be inclined to regard Hulme's poem as insubstantial – but it is remarkable how this image of the moon as a red-faced farmer remains in the mind. This poem teaches us the suggestive power of the image. We remember the image, in part, because of its sheer unexpectedness – a moon is not normally compared to a farmer, whatever the farmer's complexion might be. The moon's face seems to lean out of the poem – the image draws attention to itself as an image. The poem depends, naturally enough, on the images stored in the reader's mental library. In order to visualize it, we will need to know what farmers look like, and what people look like as they lean over hedges.

We might be inclined to construct a little narrative around the image. This is something which imagistic poems encourage us to do because, by themselves, they usually provide very little commentary. If we were to imagine this poem as written by Robert Frost, we would probably expect Frost to make something quite different of a farmer leaning over a fence – we would expect the farmer to say something and, likewise, we would expect the speaker of the poem to attempt conversation with him (indeed a scenario of this sort is played out in Frost's poem 'Mending Wall'). But Hulme's speaker emphatically does not say anything, indeed he makes a point of this: 'I did not stop to speak'. You might object that in any case the speaker cannot in any meaningful sense address the moon, however much like a farmer it appears. But the image of the farmer is such a strong one that we might feel that the speaker could hold, at least, an imaginary conversation with him. Speculations of this sort are just that – speculations. We are, though, encouraged by the final image of the stars to construct further relationships around the central image – Hulme introduces the idea of the town children whose white and unweathered faces are in contrast with the face of the imaginary farmer. We do not hear what such town children might be doing, or what the speaker thinks of them – as part of the image they are 'trusted' to resonate beside the other parts. Of course, the various parts of the image are not randomly chosen. If we look closely, we see that the poem is structured to present a series of parallel relationships: town/country; moon/stars; age/youth; red/white. The reader is left to make something of these relationships with only the slightest of nudges from the writer.

Even less commentary is on display in David Gascoyne's 'The Very Image'. In this poem we find a somewhat schematic example of one image being played off against another. Because the poem is dedicated to Magritte, Gascoyne has a convenient reason to present us with images in the style of the Surrealist painter:

THE VERY IMAGE

An image of my grandmother
her head appearing upside-down upon a cloud
the cloud transfixed on the steeple
of a deserted railway station
far away

An image of an aqueduct
with a dead crow hanging from the first arch
a modern-style chair from the second
a fir-tree lodged in the third
and the whole scene sprinkled with snow

An image of the piano tuner
with a basket of prawns on his shoulder
and a firescreen under his arm
his moustache made of clay-clotted twigs
and his cheeks daubed with wine

An image of an aeroplane
the propeller is rashers of bacon

> the wings are of reinforced lard
> the tail is made of paperclips
> the pilot is a wasp
>
> An image of the painter
> with his left hand in a bucket
> and his right hand stroking a cat
> as he lies in bed
> with a stone beneath his head
>
> And all these images
> and many others
> are arranged like waxworks
> in model birdcages
> about six inches high[2]

We float through the poem as through an art gallery. Although there are hints of the kind of contrast which we saw in Hulme's poem, Gascoyne's imagery is less obviously integrated and it forces us to make larger leaps of imagination. It is the consistently unexpected quality of the images – their unique visual style – which holds the poem together.

Reading through the poem for the first time, what will probably strike us most forcibly is the ending. The poem suddenly reduces the images in scale – as though looking through the wrong end of a telescope – so that what appeared to be life-size becomes toy-like. This is a particularly powerful move in a poem which depends so much on what the reader imagines in their mind's eye. The relations in the poem are suddenly over-turned, seen in a different light. Partly, I think, this is a way for the poem to comment on itself (the six images are reflected in the six inches of the cages). The poet reminds us that he retains artistic control, that he is a stand-in for the painter. The final image is a kind of joke, showing us how one surrealist image, like a hungry fish, can swallow another.

In the introduction to this book, I mentioned that something energetic happens when we travel to the word 'donkey' via the word 'orange'. Gascoyne's poem depends almost exclusively on this kind of energy. The movement of images in the first stanza alone is a good example. While the first line could easily belong in a conventional poem, the reader is quickly made aware that they have entered a world where different rules apply. How often do we think of the head of a relative upside down? We might stretch to give the image a realistic explanation, perhaps imagine that while the speaker is lying down and looking up at the sky, his grandmother comes over and looks down at him. But the last two lines force us to read the images in a non-realistic, associative way. We might, for example, read the image of the grandmother upside down as a reminder of a body laid out for a funeral. The association with death would then be picked up by the cloud (afterlife) and the steeple (funeral). Certainly, it is notable how each line forces us to change our view, and our reading, of the images that have gone before – every image forces us to shuffle again in our minds the pre-ceding ones. Though only two words long, the last line of the stanza forces a radical shift of viewpoint and sets up the reversal of the last stanza.

One device which Gascoyne uses to maintain a consistent visual style in the poem is to make each image seems like a construction, a piece of architecture. With respect to each image all of the parts *connect*, nothing floats free. The aqueduct, piano tuner, aeroplane and painter are like hat-stands on which improbable images are hung. The effect can be compared to asking a man to juggle, play the violin and ride a unicycle all at once. As the poet piles on the improbabilities, the reader wants to see how much weight each construction can bear. This in turn mirrors the construction of the poem as a whole – a construction which brings its unlikely parts together, just short of a collapse.

Gascoyne's speaker is relatively invisible in the poem – his presence is implied in the zany arrangements (somebody must be responsible) but the speaker does not stop to query, or otherwise to pass judgement on, his images. But this is exactly what Jorie Graham does – with great single-mindedness – in her poem 'Notes on the Reality of the Self'. Graham's poems, which are among the most compelling being written today (we will see another in the chapter on 'Variety'), often reflect on the act of looking. The poems frequently produce a number of sharp images which are then taken apart, scrutinized and reconstructed in the poet's mind. Whereas Gascoyne leaves his images alone, Graham does just the opposite. Graham's poems are, in part, meditations on what it is to use imagery in a poem.

NOTES ON THE REALITY OF THE SELF

Watching the river, each handful of it closing over the next,
brown and swollen. Oaklimbs,
gnawed at by waterfilm, lifted, relifted, lapped-at all day in
this dance of non-discovery. All things are
possible. Last year's leaves, coming unstuck from shore,

rippling suddenly again with the illusion,
and carried, twirling, shiny again and fat,
towards the quick throes of another tentative
conclusion, bobbing, circling in little suctions their stiff presence
on the surface compels. Nothing is virtual.
The long brown throat of it sucking up from some faraway melt.
Expression pouring forth, all content no meaning.
The force of it and the thingness of it identical.
Spit forth, licked up, snapped where the force
exceeds the weight, clickings, pockets.
A long sigh through the land, an exhalation.
I let the dog loose in this stretch. Crocus
appear in the gassy dank leaves. Many
earth gasses, rot gasses.
I take them in, breath at a time, I put my
breath back out
onto the scented immaterial. How the invisible
roils. I see it from here and then
I see it from here. Is there a new way of looking –
valences and little hooks – inevitabilities, proba-
bilities? It flaps and slaps. Is this body the one
I know as me? How private these words? And these? Can you
smell it, brown with little froths at the rot's lips,
meanwhiles and meanwhiles thawing then growing soggy then
the filaments where leaf-matter accrued round a
pattern, a law, slipping off, precariously, bit by bit,
and flicks, and swiftnesses suddenly more water than not.
The nature of goodness the mind exhales.
I see myself. I am a widening angle of
and *nevertheless* and *this performance has rapidly* –
nailing each point and then each next right point, interlocking, correct, correct again, each rightness snapping loose,
floating, hook in the air, swirling, seed-down,
quick – *the evidence of the visual henceforth* – and henceforth, loosening –[3]

As a student of film (she studied with Martin Scorsese), Graham's poems
are usually very self-conscious about the kinds of visual imagery which they
use. This poem is no exception. If we ask ourselves what the subject-
matter of the poem is, then we immediately find ourselves unpicking,
strand by strand, a dense web of relationships. We might begin with the
assumption that the poem is about a river – or, perhaps, the movement of
the river – but as the first word of the poem indicates the subject-matter

is at least as much the *watching* of the river. What Gascoyne's poem implies, Graham's poem makes explicit: an image is a collaboration. It is not just a matter of the poet being a camera and simply turning her head this way and that like a lens. An image is made as much by the watcher as the watched. Nor is the image an event which takes place purely, or even primarily, in the eyes. Graham's poem makes a strenuous effort to show the involvement of the watcher's whole body in what she sees.

This is a good illustration of a point once made by John Dewey:

> In seeing a picture, it is not true that visual qualities are as such, or con-sciously, central, and other qualities arranged about them in an accessory or associated fashion. Nothing could be further from the truth. It is no more true of seeing a picture than it is of reading a poem or a treatise on philo-sophy, in which we are not aware in any distinct way of the visual forms of letters and words. These are stimuli to which we respond with emotional, imaginative, and intellectual values drawn from ourselves, which are then ordered by interaction with those presented through the medium of words.[4]

Dewey reminds us that we respond to visual and verbal suggestions with our whole selves. We do not create images with the eye, but with material drawn from many different parts of our being. Graham's poem seems to be in pursuit of a wholeness which it knows it will not find. Here is one way of looking at her train of thought. What would a complete image of the river look like? If we never look into the same river twice, how can one image stand for the river in all its phases? From what possible standpoint – from underneath? Above? From one side or the other? – would such an image be composed? There is no final answer to these questions because a complete image is impossible. But that does not render the search point-less, or discourage the mind from making finer and finer images. The images which Graham *does* make available to us are necessarily partial – the handfuls of water, the oaklimbs, the proliferating leaves. In each case, our minds can readily supply images for what is being described, just as our minds, like hers, can readily become self-conscious about that process of description. Each of these images is, so to speak, stained with thought, 'the quick throes of another tentative / conclusion', with suggestions that come from other parts of her being.

For example, when she describes – vividly – the leaf-matter which is cling-ing to the bank, she uses the surprising word 'law'. Certainly, this abstrac-tion seems to parachute in from another level of thought and we may feel that it looks out of place. But is it? Does not the breakdown of matter amount to a law of nature? Is it not entirely plausible that a mind brooding on the bits and pieces found alongside a river would think about the enduring principle of decay? The word draws more attention to itself because it is placed next to a combination of words – 'slipping off, precariously' – which seem better suited to a description of physical actions rather than of conceptual processes. Although the language blurs the concrete and the abstract, the mind remains capable of producing mental images for this scene. Even when Graham converts 'meanwhile' into a noun – and a plural one at that – and assigns physical actions to these imaginary objects, readers are still able to supply appropriate images. What Graham shows us is that imagery is not just a matter of isolating an object and nailing it down with a precise description. Images can arise as readily from a train of thought, or even from the collision of two distinct trains of thought. It is not simply a matter of mimicking what we think a still or moving camera does. It is the pattern of relationships between different strands of thought which matter.

Since most of our sensual perception is visual, it is not surprising that images can work so powerfully on our minds. Your assignment is to write a poem which communicates mainly through its images. Especially look for images which have a clear, distinct quality, or else a powerfully suggestive quality, such that they render an explanation unnecessary. The presence of an I-persona and all narrative commentary should be minimal.

Notes

1   Patrick McGuinness, ed., *T. E. Hulme: Selected Writings* (Manchester: Carcanet, 2003), p. 1.
2   Robin Skelton, ed., *Poetry of the Thirties* (London: Penguin, 1964), pp. 234–5.
3   Jorie Graham, *The Dream of the Unified Field: Selected Poems* (Manchester: Carcanet, 1996), pp. 159–60.
4   John Dewey, *Art as Experience*, 1st edn. 1934 (New York: Perigree, 1980), p. 123.

7

Short Lines

In this chapter and the next I want to discuss line-length. Rather than examine rhythm as a separate topic, I think it is best to discuss it in the context of the length of the line. Given that some of our discussion in these two chapters will focus on the distribution of stressed syllables from line to line, it is as well to explain the relevant terminology.

A poem's rhythm is usually analysed in terms of its metrical structure, which in turn depends on the concept of the foot. The poetic foot consists of a small number of syllables in the line, usually two or three. Different kinds of poetic foot give rise to different kinds of rhythm. There are four major types of foot in the poetic line. First, the iamb: this consists of an unstressed syllable followed by a stressed syllable. An example is the word 'motel'. Second, the trochee: this consists of a stressed syllable followed by an unstressed syllable. An example is the word 'model'. If you repeat the words 'model' and 'motel', you should immediately see the difference in stress pattern. Third, the anapaest: this consists of two unstressed syllables followed by a stressed one. An example is the word 'denigrate'. Fourth, the dactyl: this consists of a stressed syllable followed by two unstressed ones. An example is the word 'editor'. All four types of foot are associated with a certain kind of rhythm. An iambic line has a rising rhythm ('I want to teach the world to sing') while a trochaic line has a falling rhythm ('twenty farmers left last summer'). An anapaestic line has a rhythm which rises faster (a spiralling upward effect) while a dactylic line has a rhythm which falls faster (a spiralling downward effect).

Here are two examples of these rhythms, both of which are taken from the poems of Yeats. A common way to mark the pattern of stressed and unstressed syllables is to mark an unstressed syllable with an 'x' and to mark a stressed syllable with a '/'. Here is Yeats's poem 'To A Squirrel at Kyle-na-no':

```
    x   /   x   /
Come play with me;
    x   /   x   /
Why should you run
    x       x / x   /
Through the shaking tree
  x   /   x x   /
As though I'd a gun
  x   /   x   /
To strike you dead?
    x  / x  x      /
When all I would do
x x   /      x   /
Is to scratch your head
  x  /  x  /
And let you go.¹
```

One can mark this entire short-line poem as a combination of iambic and anapaestic feet, with no more or fewer than two feet in every line. Mostly, the poem is iambic, which accounts for its light, lilting rhythm. Note that metre and rhythm are not exactly the same thing. The metre influences the rhythm, but the rhythm is also influenced by elements like syntax, tone and diction. Here is the beginning of quite a different poem, 'The Fiddler of Dooney', again with the pattern of stressed and unstressed syllables marked out:

```
    x   x   /   x   x   /   x x   /     x
When I play on my fiddle in Dooney
  x   /   x   x /   x x   /
Folk dance like a wave of the sea
  x  /    x x   /    x  x / x
My cousin is priest in Kilvarnet
  x  /   x  x /   x    /
My brother in Mocharabuiee²
```

Again the rhythm is a rising one, but in this case there are more anapaestic than iambic feet in the verse. This is another way of saying that there is a higher proportion of unstressed syllables, and as these create less 'resistance' when we read, the impression is that the verse here reads faster. The underlying anapaestic beat creates an impression of energetic, swinging movement which fits with the descriptions of music and dancing in these lines.

While it is very useful to know these four basic types (there are other types much less useful to know) one need not fetishize any of them. A poem is not necessarily improved by giving it a regular iambic structure – indeed, it may be considerably disimproved. These patterns are better thought of as useful signposts which help us to analyse certain effects in a poem. By and large, a poem will earn effects by varying rhythm rather than by slavishly maintaining one. A poem with an unvarying rhythm approaches the condition of a nursery rhyme, emphatic rhythms being easier for children to absorb. Often, it can be hard, in any given line, to work out an exact stress-pattern. What is important, however, is that a writer has a general rhythmic awareness. There is a fine passage in the work of Kenneth Burke where he discusses the relationship between the rhythm and the sense of the writer's words. Burke is talking about prose rhythms but what he says is also instructive for poetry:

> A reader sensitive to prose rhythms is like a man hurrying through a crowd; at one time he must halt, at another time he can leap forward; he darts perilously between saunterers; he guards himself in turning sharp corners. We mean that in all rhythmic experiences one's 'muscular imagination' is touched. Similarly with sounds, there is some analogy to actual movement, since sounds may rise and fall, and in a remote way one rises and falls with them.[3]

In this chapter, then, we will look at the effects of short lines on the rhythm of the poem, as well as other possibilities which are latent in this form.

Because a line-break creates a pause, short-line poems, in general, read more slowly than those with long lines. For our present purposes I am defining a short-line poem as one where most of the lines contain three beats (three stresses) or fewer. Since the most popular line in English literature is the iambic pentameter (containing five beats), historically speaking, short-line poems are in the minority. As well as being slower, short-line poems tend to have more heavily emphasized words as a proportion of the whole. This is because a line-break adds emphasis to the words which come immediately before and after it. Short-line poems tend to be of short length, that is to say, usually they do not contain many lines, because it can be difficult to find a topic which would justify numerous emphasized words over a prolonged period (this is one of the reasons Shakespeare did not write speeches for his characters with two- or three-beat lines). In this chapter, however, we will see an exception to this rule in the form of a short-line narrative poem by Christina Rossetti.

Because of their patterns of slowness and emphasis, short-line poems are good at conveying intricate motion, at imitating the various stages of an action. The poems of A. R. Ammons convey this effect well – note the way his poem 'Loss' (below) captures the motion of daisies moving around in the wind. The line-breaks are absolutely central to this process and the varying stress-pattern conveys the sense of being pushed around. Blake's 'The Fly' exploits the 'lightness' of short lines, creating an impression of flimsiness and vulnerability. In general, intricate sound-patterns are more noticeable in short-line poems. Poems with rich, complicated diction, like those of Sylvia Plath, for example, can exploit their short lines to emphasize unusual word-choices. The fragmentation of frequent, *irregular* line-breaks can be used, in combination with dramatic monologue, to create a sense of psychic disturbance.

In Blake's 'The Fly' we see how short lines can contribute to a general impression of flimsiness. In this poem, not only the lines but the stanzas are short:

Little Fly,
Thy summer's play
My thoughtless hand
Has brush'd away.

Am not I
A fly like thee?
Or art not thou
A man like me?

For I dance,
And drink, & sing,
Till some blind hand
Shall brush my wing.

If thought is life
And strength & breath,
And the want
Of thought is death,

Then am I
A happy fly,
If I live
Or if I die.[4]

We might say that Blake is putting short lines to their most obvious use: to create an impression of insubstantiality. Verbally, the poem creates a sense of thinness by avoiding long, broad vowels and using a high proportion of thin ones. Furthermore, the poem is overwhelmingly monosyllabic – not only are there only two stresses per line, sometimes there are only three syllables. Hence the poem seems to lack weight and body.

In a good demonstration of the use of scale, Blake reinforces our impression of the fly's smallness by having it come into contact with a human hand, a contrast which is ironically enhanced when the dimensions of the speaker are compared with the hand of a deity. Structurally, the poem also reinforces the sense of insubstantiality by a kind of communicative incompleteness. The speaker, in the second stanza, asks himself questions which he does not answer. Another unusual effect is gained by the writer placing most of the important words in the poem at the middle rather than at the ends of the lines. This emphasizes the less important words and creates an impression of modesty.

'The Fly' is mostly iambic. Apart from the first line, all the lines in the first stanza are iambic. This regularity creates a sing-song effect, the kind of emphatic regularity which one might find in a nursery rhyme. One of the instructive variations from the metre comes in line 11, 'Till some blind hand'. The stresses in this line are hard to distribute as the words carry relatively equal weight. One can, for example, read all of the words in this line as being stressed, which makes it a 'heavier' line, appropriate given that it is intended to signal the violence of the hand against the fly.

In contrast to 'The Fly', A. R. Ammons's poem about a group of daisies demonstrates a much more aggressive use of short lines. Whereas Blake's poem aims to give us a sense of the dimensions of the fly, 'Loss' aims to give us a sense of the movement of the daisies:

Loss

When the sun
falls behind the sumac
thicket the
wild

> yellow daisies
> in diffuse evening shade
> lose their
> rigorous attention,
> and
> half-wild with loss
> turn
> any way the wind does
> and lift their
> petals up
> to float
> off their stems
> and go

The emphasis here is on movement and change and only secondarily on size and substance. We might not want to claim that Ammons is out-doing Blake, but it is obvious that his poem is much more active – the reader is given the impression that they are one of the daisies being pushed about. Among the major differences between the two poems is the way in which Ammons performs his poem as a single forward motion, as one unwinding sentence without any stanza-breaks to slow the reader down. Another important difference is the use of irregular line-lengths, which creates a jerky effect, a suitable way to convey the agitation of the flowers.

'Loss' is a deceptive poem because it looks as if it was relatively easy to write. In reality, this is a finely controlled poem which pays intense attention to the weights of words and syllables. In the first place we might note the effect of changes of scale in the poem. It begins with a very large object, the sun, in order to focus on a set of much smaller objects, the wild daisies. But the sinking sun is not present merely to set the scene, or to provide an intriguing evening atmosphere. The relationship which it has to the flowers is central – it is after all what keeps the flowers alive, and it is what provokes their 'rigorous attention' – they have been following its progress all day. Ammons only mentions the sun once and yet its presence is firmly established in our minds through the clever manipulation of the short lines. The very first verb, 'falls', for example, neatly enacts the movement of the sun, not only because of the word's meaning but because as we read our eyes go down, like the sun, to the next line. As well as that, by placing the verb at the beginning of a line, Ammons has increased its force. At the end of the same line, and at the beginning of the next, we encounter the phrase 'sumac / thicket'. 'Sumac' is the first unusual word in the poem and also introduces us to the first harsh syllable, a syllable which is further picked up by the first syllable of 'thicket'. Verbally speaking, it is the first 'obstruc-tion' which we encounter in the poem, and neatly parallels the way the sumac thicket (the first syllable of this is also hard to burrow through) obstructs the relationship between the sun and the daisies.

One of the clever variations in the poem is the type of word used at the start of the each line. In the first three lines, for example, the sequence of head-words is conjunction, verb, noun. This adds to the verbal interest of the next word in the pattern, a word which also happens to stand alone, the adjective 'wild'. As I shall explain, this is an intriguing word from many points of view. The word conveys a sense of instability because it comes between the definite article and its noun – when we see 'the' sitting at the end of the line we might reasonably expect whatever word comes next to be a noun. Indeed, reading the poem for the first time we will not be sure until we travel over yet another line-break whether or not 'wild' is a noun here (it can be).

Given a whole line to itself, the word 'wild' has to do a lot of work. In general it can be dangerous to rely on one-word lines, just as it can be fool-ish to rely on using block capitals. Such lines confer enormous emphasis on the words they isolate. In this case, Ammons uses a word he will later repeat, or at least half-repeat (although it doesn't carry the same mean-ing both times). 'Wild' is what we might call a 'poetic' adjective, the sort of word we associate with the popular notion of what poetry should be about: free, unconstrained, impossible to tame. When Ammons uses the word for the first time, it is in a prosaic horticultural sense, as a way of distinguishing what kind of flowers these are. The second time he uses the word, however, it is closer to the more exciting 'poetic' sense of 'wild', although even in this case he swerves away from cliché by using the compound 'half-wild'. We might say that there is a correspondence between the first ordinary meaning and the biological fact of the daisies, while the second meaning reminds us that the flowers have been anthropomorphized. What these subtle effects demonstrate is that short-line poems encourage an intense relationship between words and line-breaks, and particularly they encourage us to think about words on their own or in relation to only one or two of their fellows.

'Goblin Market' by Christina Rossetti offers us an intriguing example of a narrative poem in short lines. Here is its opening:

GOBLIN MARKET

Morning and evening
Maids heard the goblins cry:
'Come buy our orchard fruits,
Come buy, come buy:
Apples and quinces,
Lemons and oranges,
Plump unpecked cherries,
Melons and raspberries,
Bloom-down-cheeked peaches,
Swart-headed mulberries,
Wild free-born cranberries,
Crab-apples, dewberries,
Pine-apples, blackberries,
Apricots, strawberries; –
All ripe together
In summer weather, –
Morns that pass by,
Fair eves that fly;
Come buy, come buy;
Our grapes fresh from the vine,
Pomegranates full and fine,
Dates and sharp bullaces,
Rare pears and greengages,
Damsons and bilberries,
Taste them and try:
Currants and gooseberries,
Bright-fire-like barberries,
Figs to fill your mouth,
Citrons from the South,
Sweet to tongue and sound to eye,
Come buy, come buy.'

Evening by evening
Among the brookside rushes,
Laura bowed her head to hear,
Lizzie veiled her blushes:
Crouching close together
In the cooling weather,
With clasping arms and cautioning lips,
With tingling cheeks and finger-tips.

'Lie close,' Laura said,
Pricking up her golden head:
'We must not look at goblin men,
We must not buy their fruits:
Who knows upon what soil they fed
Their hungry thirsty roots?'[5]

Short lines can be difficult to use for narrative and Rossetti solves this problem by making a virtue of their limitations. In particular, 'Goblin Market' makes use of a hypnotic, repetitive rhythm which suits the dream/nightmare scenario it describes. Unlike those of Ammons's 'Loss', the lines in this poem have a sing-song regularity, even though the number of stresses varies from two to four. Rossetti uses a trochaic rhythm in which the first syllable of the line is usually stressed. The sense of regularity is partly established by a heavy reliance on feminine endings (when the last syllable of a line is unstressed, we call this a 'feminine ending'). The list of fruits which the goblins offer for sale is almost exclusively made up of lines of this sort, and this rhythmical motif is sharply underlined by the similar shape of the words, the way in which so many of these names end in '-berries'. A further rhythmical motif is established by using pairs throughout the poem: 'Morning and evening' has the same rhythmical shape as 'Apples and quinces' and as the names of the girls, Lizzie and Laura. The unstressed 'and' in the middle of many of the lines helps to pattern the lines, too, because the syllable which follows it is usually stressed. When the expected 'and' disappears for a while after line 8, we still register its absence in the slightly quicker lines that follow. The most striking repeated line is also the goblin's ultimate appeal 'Come buy, come buy', an unusual line because all the syllables bear a stress. The emphatic effect of this is of a bell-like insistence – making this a line which we are waiting for through the rest of the poem.

The opening of the poem puts us in the position of the two girls who will be tempted by the goblin fruit. Look at the minimal space which Rossetti devotes to exposition. We are not told where we are, who the girls are, what sort of world this is. Consequently, when the goblins begin their sales-pitch we are in much the same position as the two girls, receiving this strange invitation as if out of nowhere. We are given no time to distance ourselves from the action and so detailed, so sensuous, is the menu that we are rapidly persuaded of the reality of this world, by the very words which tempt Lizzie and Laura. The narrator is only a shadowy presence. It would be easy for a narrator to intrude too much on this story, offering suggestions to the

reader as to how the tale is to be received, but Rossetti's narrator lets the
speech of her characters dominate so that we are free to make up our own
minds about them. Instead it is the rhythm which suggests how we should
receive the material. For example, the trochaic pulse shifts to an iambic
rhythm when Laura is speaking, suggesting a conflict between her view of
things and that of the goblins. Because the rhythm has mostly been falling,
the rising rhythm of Laura's speech sounds even more anxious than it would
in a mostly iambic poem.

By way of concluding this chapter, I want to look at one of my own short-
line poems. It is a relatively light poem about two cats who live together
even though they don't get on. Here is one of the early drafts:

DOUBLE FELIX

Her fur is for
portraiture.

His purr is far
more appreciative.

Pure comparison
makes a pair of them.

Not the compared –
together they stare

apart, their pursuits
are separate: sloth

(hers); ladybugs,
dust and her (his).

Nightly he pursues
her – but for fun . . .

nothing further.

The poem is already not far from its finished state, although it would progress
through another five versions. The opening and ending are already in place
in this draft but there are considerable problems in the middle section.

Reading through this draft, some of the effects of using short lines are quite noticeable. One of the most prominent is the emphasis placed on words other than nouns or verbs. An example of this is the near-rhyme of 'for' and 'far', two mundane words which might not ordinarily attract much attention. At the same time, the line-break associated with both words is augmented by a parallel emphasis on the word immediately following in the next line: 'for' and the first syllable of 'portraiture', 'far' and 'more'. This is typical of the kind of close sonic effects one can achieve within a short-line poem. The poem is short enough for the writer to make use of 'vertical connections', as words resonate with the sound of others not on the same line. All of the words we have looked at chime with what we might call the 'key words' of the poem: 'purr' and 'fur'. This is a light-hearted poem and it is not above playing with words with such obvious feline associations.

The poem presents us with a pair of cats, a kind of dysfunctional married couple, and, in a more than casual way, it has been organized into couplets in order to reflect this. Because the poem wants to suggest closeness without harmony, intimacy without union, from the beginning it does not flow. The opening line invites the reader to ask, *why break the line here?* The word 'for' suggests it is to be followed by a useful revelation – why should the reader not hear what the cat's fur is for in the opening line? By withholding this information, for the slight but significant time in which we travel over the line-break, the poem suggests that it is playing with us and creates an impression of resistance. Augmenting this sense is the staccato effect created by the first two statements. The statements are linked – one can't fully understand the second without the first – and yet the rhythm and syntax suggest that they are separated. The ends of the first two sentences coincide with the ends of the first two couplets and, each time, this makes for a very emphatic pause, a sense (if I might echo the language of my own poem) of thus far and no further.

As I mentioned previously, there are problems with this version of the poem, and among its words and phrases are a number of candidates for revision. The third couplet, for example, stumbles rhythmically. In line 5, the word 'pure' suggested itself for sonic reasons, but it is not obvious what it contributes as a modifier for 'comparison'. Sonically, line 6 is questionable. It is OK to use a colloquial phrase such as 'Makes a pair of them' in a poem which is casually idiomatic. But it is not OK to have a line which contains three stresses and to place yet another stress at the beginning of the line. Together these two lines dissipate the staccato force stored up by the opening.

The fourth couplet is also defective. 'Not the compared' is an awkward way for the speaker to expand on his point and is a good illustration of the kind of tortured, twisted expressions which short lines can invite. The poem is already starting to depart from the kind of natural expressions we could plausibly expect the speaker to use. The expression is also a little bit too emphatic, as though the speaker were on the verge of losing their cool. On the other hand, the invented expression 'stare apart', which plays with more common expressions like 'stare out' and 'set apart', seems like a good idea, especially split up by a double line-break, and this was something which I preserved through subsequent drafts.

As I worked on improving the poem, the drafts show that I was trying to do something with the word 'pure'. Initially, I replaced it with the word 'brief', which is at least a move in the right sonic direction. Eventually, I hit on the word 'rough', which, ironically, has a meaning almost opposite to 'pure'. 'Rough comparison' seemed better, though, more in keeping with the sense that the poem is a kind of sketch, a quick glance of appraisal. Also 'rough' has the considerable benefit of reversing the sound of 'fur' (if you try to say this word backwards you will see what I mean) and so fits in nicely with the poem's sonic pattern. Having incorporated this critical change, the poem's direction became much clearer. Here is the final version of the poem:

DOUBLE FELIX

Her fur is for
portraiture.

His purr is far
more appreciative.

Rough comparison
effects a pair –

togetherness –
as of two paws,

while, side by side,
the compared stare

apart, their pursuits
separate: sloth

(hers); ladybugs,
dust and her (his).

All night he pursues
her, but for fun . . .

nothing further.

Your assignment is to write a poem with short lines. Not all the lines need to be short, but most of them should have three beats or fewer. Try to create effects with words like 'in', 'an', 'this' and 'there' which often go unnoticed in poems with longer lines. Also take the opportunity to draw out vertical connections, of the sort described in this chapter, between significant words.

Notes

1   W. B. Yeats, *The Collected Poems of W. B. Yeats*, 1st edn. 1933, 2nd edn. 1950 (London: Macmillan, 1982), p. 175.
2   Yeats, *The Collected Poems*, p. 82.
3   Kenneth Burke, *Counter-Statement* (Berkeley, Los Angeles, London: University of California Press, 1968), p. 141.
4   Peter Butter, ed., *William Blake: Selected Poems* (London: Everyman, 1996), p. 33.
5   Christopher Ricks, ed., *The New Oxford Book of Victorian Verse* (Oxford and New York: Oxford University Press, 1987), pp. 284–5.

8

Long Lines

When a writer swerves away from the default poetic model, the swerve itself is a potential source of energy. By comparison to the default four- or five-beat line in English, the long line necessarily gives the impression of containing additional material, of having something more to enfold or impart. A reader who is used to four- or five-beat lines is likely to wonder what the extra elements in the line are for. The best long-line poems exploit this sense of the superfluous. Poems with long lines frequently contain catalogues, often bringing together a large number of objects within a relatively small space. Poems of this sort are particularly useful to poets who like to proceed by accumulation, adding one detail to another in order to create an intricate picture. Long-line poems often tend to be superior to their short-line cousins in conveying a narrative because there is more room within the long line for connective parts of speech, for coordinating qualifications and clarifications.

Long-line poems are favoured by poets – one thinks immediately of D. H. Lawrence and Walt Whitman – with idiosyncratic poetic voices. Again, this is because of the permissive nature of the long line; it allows such poets to include those elements – repetitions, exclamations, digressions – which mark out the individuality of a voice. The effect can be made to seem very natural, as though we were listening to a story in a bar. Long-line poems have relatively few emphasized words, so they are good for subtle, under- stated narrative styles, such as we find illustrated in this chapter by their best-known contemporary exponent, C. K. Williams.

Regular long-line poems can occasionally be emphatic in their rhythms, although this is difficult to maintain over long periods. Here is an exam- ple by Thomas Hardy which uses emphatic rhythms:

THROWING A TREE
(NEW FOREST)

The two executioners stalk along over the knolls,
Bearing two axes with heavy heads shining and wide,
And a long limp two-handled saw toothed for cutting great boles,
And so they approach the proud tree that bears the death-mark on its side.

Jackets doffed they swing axes and chop away just above ground,
And the chips fly about and lie white on the moss and fallen leaves;
Till a broad deep gash in the bark is hewn all the way round,
And one of them tries to hook upward a rope, which at last he achieves.

The saw then begins, till the top of the tall giant shivers:
The shivers are seen to grow greater each cut than before:
They edge out the saw, tug the rope; but the tree only quivers,
And kneeling and sawing again, they step back to try pulling once more.

Then, lastly, the living mast sways, further sways: with a shout
Job and Ike rush aside. Reached the end of its long staying powers
The tree crashes downward: it shakes all its neighbours throughout,
And two hundred years' steady growth has been ended in less than two hours.[1]

Mainly through his handling of the line, Hardy manages to create a remarkable sense of sinister energy. It is the kind of energy which the sensitive reader would like to deflect from the tree. There is not much plot in the poem. It simply records the destruction of one tree. Beyond their names, we are never given any details about the two men who are cutting it down, so the poem is dependent on other sources – line-length being one of these – to absorb the reader's interest.

Hardy establishes an anapaestic rhythm in the long lines – and this very energetic beat is played off against other elements. Hardy is good at making the tumbling forward momentum of the anapaests conflict with the language and syntax, so that we have a sense of energy encountering tough resistance, just as the saw is resisted by the bole of the tree. In the fifth line, for example, the anapaestic pulse is particularly marked, and is emphasized by verbal echoes which occur within the line: the way in which the word 'doffed', for instance, is echoed by another prominently stressed word, 'chop'. As this stanza develops, the rhythm is maintained in order to give the reader the feel of unimpeded activity. Only in the last line, where a comma marks off a subordinate clause, is the rhythm interrupted – at the point where the men commence another part of their task.

One of the major points of tension occurs in the seventh line. The anapaestic beat encourages us to place a stress on the word 'all' rather than on the word 'hewn'. But 'hewn', being the active part of the sentence, must bear a certain amount of stress. When these pressures are combined the reader feels a 'pull' in two directions, a force which reminds the reader uncomfortably of how the tree is torn. If one were able to isolate this line and read it as the opening of a poem we would place the stresses differently – the line would read awkwardly and we might be inclined to place a caesura, or break, after 'hewn', dividing the line into two comfortable pieces.

In music, when a note is sustained for an unusual period of time, listeners become increasingly expectant, their minds directed towards the point when the note will stop. Similarly, in poems with lines of unusual length, readers directs their minds forward to the point where the line will break, and inevitably this creates tension. C. K. Williams is well known as a specialist practitioner of the long line, and in his poem 'Instinct' we seem him building tension by these means, enhancing the effect through the poem's syntax:

INSTINCT

Although he's apparently the youngest (his little rasta-beard is barely
    down and feathers),
most casually connected (he hardly glances at the girl he's with, though
    she might be his wife),
half-sloshed (or more than half) on picnic-whiskey teen-aged father,
    when his little son,
two or so, tumbles from the slide, hard enough to scare himself, hard
    enough to make him cry,
really cry, not partly cry, not pretend the fright for what must be some
    scarce attention,
but really let it out, let loudly be revealed the fear of having been so close
    to real fear,
he, the father, knows just how quickly he should pick the child up, then
    how firmly hold it,
fit its head into the muscled socket of his shoulder, rub its back, croon
    and whisper to it,
and finally pull away a little, about a head's length, looking, still
    concerned, into its eyes,

then smiling, broadly, brightly, as though something had been shared,
   something of importance,
not dreadful, or not very, not at least now that it's past, but rather
   something . . . funny,
funny, yes, it was funny, wasn't it, to fall and cry like that, though one
   certainly can understand,
we've all had glimpses of a premonition of the anguish out there, you're
   better now, though,
aren't you, why don't you go back and try again, I'll watch you, maybe
   have another drink,
yes, my son, my love, I'll go back and be myself now: you go be the
   person you are, too.[2]

As even the most casual reader is likely to see, this poem is a single long sentence. When experienced over the course of so many long lines, there is a danger, given the syntactic structure, that the poem will seem too wordy, and its story too drawn-out. Certainly, the length of the sentence, and of the lines, makes the reader aware of the need to stop, the need to break the flow. My own view is that defeating the expectation of a resting-place works in the poem's favour.

Williams's diction is carefully colloquial. His subject-matter is recognizably down-to-earth. It is the kind of contemporary urban scene any of us may have witnessed. The overall effect of these features, combined with the long lines, is of listening to somebody very articulate engage in intimate conversation, over a café table perhaps. We can all think of people who talk in just this way, spelling everything out, qualifying lots of phrases, attempting to be precise. It is like listening to someone talk, while at the same time we can see that they are listening to themselves. This gives the long line an exploratory quality – consider the moment when the speaker hits on the adjective 'funny'. As the word is repeated, we experience the speaker testing its rightness, looking at it from a number of angles, then deciding that it will do. To experience the moment when the speaker finds the right word makes the reader feel as though they have access to the poem's formation – the speaker seems to be more on our level, prepared to show us how he has reached his conclusions. In this context, the long lines appear to be like feelers which the speaker gradually extends towards the unfolding scene. As in Hardy's poem, not a great deal happens, but unlike Hardy's poem, this has drama that lies in what the speaker makes of the scene. In Hardy's poem, we become part of the action – and this magnifies the event, whereas in Williams's poem we become part of the drama of

thinking about the action. Because of that, to take out any of the qualifications in the poem – for example, the parentheses towards the beginning
– would be to remove something essential. Although the qualifications do
not advance the action of the poem – in fact, they retard it – they do allow
us to follow the flow of the speaker's thinking.

In contrast to Williams's poem, Ciaran Carson's 'Bloody Hand' frequently
interrupts the natural flow of the long line:

BLOODY HAND

Your man, says the Man, will walk into the bar like this – here his fingers
Mimic a pair of legs, one stiff at the knee – so you'll know exactly
What to do. He sticks a finger to his head. Pretend it's child's play –
The hand might be a horse's mouth, a rabbit or a dog. Five handclaps.
Walls have ears: the shadows you throw are the shadows you try to throw
      off.

I snuff out the candle between finger and thumb. Was it the left hand
Hacked off at the wrist and thrown to the shores of Ulster? Did Ulster
Exist? Or the Right Hand of God, saying Stop to this and No to that?
My thumb is the hammer of a gun. The thumb goes up. The thumb goes
      down.[3]

Like Hardy's poem, 'Bloody Hand' shows how effective long lines can
be at conveying a repetitive action, particularly one which the reader
might prefer to stop. In this poem, Carson uses metonymy (substitution
of part for whole) to encourage sinister imagery in the reader's mind. The
speaker appears to be a hitman who has received instructions to undertake a killing (the reader may like to know that the symbol of Ulster is a
red hand, which according to myth its owner cut off and threw to shore
in order to win a sea-race and claim the land). This is a poem in which
much remains undisclosed. Our minds come to rest only on body-parts –
hand, thumb, finger, mouth, leg, knee. We are left to guess what is hidden
in the darkness, what the owners of these parts might look like. To adapt
a phrase of the painter Paul Klee's, we might say that Carson takes the long
line for a walk in the form of a hand. As the line extends, we imagine this
animal-like hand creeping across the page. Carson's stated intention with
this line-length was to give the sense of a traditional Irish storyteller (the
lines are usually not self-contained, you are forced to go on to the next
one to make sense of the last).

In some respects this is a poem which reads quickly. Around the third line, we seem to shift abruptly from one environment to another. The jumps from sentence to sentence are not always clear. If we contrast this poem with 'Instinct', the major difference we find is that Carson breaks the poem into a large number of sentences. Whereas Williams allowed his one sentence to contain fifteen lines, Carson allows one of his lines to contain three sentences. Whereas the lines in 'Instinct' augmented the sense of a long drawn-out action, an action which was being pondered from numerous points of view, 'Bloody Hand' depends on a conflict between the sentences and the lines, as a dangerous action is insufficiently pondered. Carson's sentences are more surprising because the mind of the speaker is troubled, and unable to focus on the issues which have disturbed it. Once we have the opening image in our mind, the unstoppable march of the murderous hand counterpoints the unstructured thoughts of the speaker, just as the long lines counterpoint the short, jabby sentences.

Your assignment is to write a poem with long lines. For the purpose of this exercise that means that most of the lines should contain twelve syllables or more. Try to make use of the opportunity to include 'extra' words in the line, perhaps to include conversational markers or to include lists of objects. In order to convey a sense of the extra, try to choose a subject, or situation, about which you have more than enough to say.

Notes

1 James Gibson, ed., *The Variorum Edition of the Complete Poems of Thomas Hardy* (London: Macmillan, 1979), p. 857.
2 C. K. Williams, *New & Selected Poems* (Newcastle: Bloodaxe, 1995), p. 259.
3 Ciaran Carson, *Belfast Confetti* (Loughcrew: Gallery, 1989), p. 51.

9

Diction

The English language is a rich and varied instrument. The flexibility of its literature is partly due to its remarkable ability to absorb new words from other languages. As the various invasions of Britain since the time of the Romans left their mark, the language bears testimony to Latin, German, French and Scandinavian influences. In the wake of the British Empire, and with the spread of American culture, it is now the main global language, absorbing an even greater range of loan-words. For poets, this variety is a great opportunity.

As we all know, when we write a job-letter or a chatty email we use words of a different type according to context. Even when words have roughly the same meaning, their effect will be very different if they belong to a colloquial register or to an elevated one. We may, for example, choose to describe a poor person either as 'skint' or as 'destitute'. We may choose to describe a drunk person either as 'smashed' or as 'inebriated'. Official documents favour more elevated word-choices, tending towards a poly-syllabic Latinate vocabulary. When we wish to appear 'sophisticated' we may use words like 'boudoir', 'debonair' and 'risqué', a Frenchified vocab-ulary which reflects the fact that, during the Norman-French invasion of England, French was the language of the ruling class. More forthright, mono-syllabic, 'no-nonsense' word-choices often reflect the Anglo-Saxon roots of English.

In poetry, richness of diction is generally achieved not by adopting a *whole-sale* Latinate or French or Anglo-Saxon vocabulary but by creating an art-ful *mixture*. Like combining patterned clothes with plain, it is a matter of relationships. More energy is usually released when words of a different register are brought together. Language use is often an opportunity for satire.

Forms of language are heavily associated with social class. A great deal of poetic energy can be released if one plays with these conventions.

Gerard Manley Hopkins is a poet who uses a noticeably rich diction – his poems often feel densely packed with exotic and unexpected word-choices. He is like a painter who arranges his subject-matter under layers and layers of thick paint. Here, by way of example, is a poem in which he turns to his favourite theme, the comforting manifestation of God in the natural world:

THAT NATURE IS A HERACLITEAN FIRE AND OF THE COMFORT OF THE RESURRECTION

Cloud-puffball, torn tufts, tossed pillows | flaunt forth, then chevy on an
    air-
Built thoroughfare: heaven-roysterers, in gay-gangs | they throng; they
    glitter in marches.
Down roughcast, down dazzling whitewash, | wherever an elm arches,
Shivelights and shadowtackle in long | lashes lace, lance, and pair.
Delightfully the bright wind boisterous | ropes, wrestles, beats earth bare
Of yestertempest's creases; | in pool and rutpeel parches
Squandering ooze to squeezed | dough, crust, dust; stanches, starches
Squadroned masks and manmarks | treadmire toil there
Footfretted in it. Million-fuelèd, | nature's bonfire burns on.
But quench her bonniest, dearest | to her, her clearest-selvèd spark
Man, how fast his firedint, | his mark on mind, is gone!
Both are in an únfathomable, all is in an enormous dark
Drowned. O pity and indig | nation! Manshape, that shone
Sheer off, disseveral, a star, | death blots black out; nor mark
            Is any of him at all so stark
But vastness blurs and time | beats level. Enough! The Resurrection,
A heart's clarion! Away grief's gasping, | joyless days, dejection.
            Across my foundering deck shone
A beacon, an eternal beam. | Flesh fade, and mortal trash
Fall to the residuary worm; | world's wildfire, leave but ash:
            In a flash, at a trumpet crash,
I am all at once what Christ is, | since he was what I am and
This Jack, joke, poor potsherd, | patch, matchwood, immortal diamond,
            Is immortal diamond.[1]

Through diction, rhythm and fragmentary images, Hopkins creates a characteristically boisterous effect. As we read, we can almost feel the poet out on a mountain, with the weather changing and the wind blowing hard. But any attempt to paraphrase the drift of this sparkling poem must come up short. How poor any paraphrase of this poem sounds. This is because Hopkins's style of language is so peculiarly his own. Change the kind of language used and the poem disappears, and Hopkins disappears with it.

Reading this for the first time, we may be put off by the intense concentration of words and thoughts. From the opening of the poem we are led into unfamiliar linguistic territory. Partly this is because Hopkins's syntax is highly elliptical. In order to approximate the excitement of ordinary speech, he likes to drop parts of the sentence which one would otherwise expect to find. Even more of the poem's difficulty is caused by the diction. Note the concentration of nouns. In the first half line (Hopkins sometimes indicated a caesura, a rhythmical break in the middle of a line, typographically), four of the six words are nouns and there are no parts of the sentence to coordinate them. When we reach the first verb, 'flaunt', we expect it to have an object – we expect the cloud-puffballs to flaunt something. Instead we are told that they 'flaunt forth', so that the entire phrase is made to mean something like 'go' or 'come'. It is worth pointing this out because we may think that the strangeness of Hopkins's poems is caused by the use of very unusual words which we may have to look up in the dictionary. Sometimes it is simply that common words are used in odd combinations. Many of these words are compounds – words which are relational in themselves, like 'Manshape' or 'firedint'. After a while, too many invented compounds will test the reader's patience, but Hopkins shows great invention in their employment. Notice the way in which learned-sounding words like 'disseveral' jostle with ordinary words arranged in close sonic patterns, like 'dough, crust, dust'. The most striking change of word-choice comes at the end of the poem. The emotional climax is heightened by the shift from the monosyllabic penultimate line to the packed compounds of the final line. We pass through a series of complicated word-choices to a series of simple ones, then back to a series of heavily stressed words, made still more emphatic by repetition. The effect is of passing through confusion, to revelation, and then to a kind of emotional clarity.

Our next example is a fine prose-poem by the Irish poet, Dennis O'Driscoll:

POULAPHOUCA RESERVOIR

Where ivy grows on a house, the family gets worn out
– The Poulaphouca Survey

1. The name 'Poulaphouca' means the hole of the spirit. Quernstones by the submerged cottages will be ground in the mills of God, fine as the distinction between Father, Son, and Holy Spirit.

2. *The Shell Guide to Ireland* calls it 'the great lake of the Liffey hydro-electric works'.

3. Life goes on in that Atlantis. Ivy grows on houses. Haws redden in autumn. Roses are pruned back. Thatch is replenished. Bridal veils float like surf on the clear-skinned water. Turf fires blaze in the lake at sunset.

4. The Field at the Bottom of the Lane is at the bottom of the lake. The Field Under the Well is under water. A school of fish chases in the School House Field. The Coarse Little Field, The Field at the Back of the House, The Inside Field are flooded permanently. Garnaranny, Farnafowluch, Carnasillogue, Coolyemoon are spoken of in bubbles.

5. During summers of drought, you can see outlines of houses. Their owners' names linger at the tip of the lake's tongue. Chimneys poke above the water like the blowholes of hunted whales.[2]

This prose-poem is clearly dependent on artful changes of language use, which the numbered paragraphs help to emphasize. In particular, the poem is balanced between a dry, factual account of the environment it describes and a more warmly sympathetic view. The speaker of the poem, if we can think of it as having a single speaker, gives little away – but much of what he gives away is a function of his word-choices.

Consider the title. The poem confronts us with a place-name which the overwhelming number of readers outside Ireland will not recognize. Few of these readers will even guess how the place-name is usually pronounced (roughly, 'pool-a-vooka'). So this proper name creates a kind of tension for the reader before the poem has even started. This tension is increased by the speaker's immediate definition of the word. As readers we are given to understand that the nature of this word, a place-name with roots in the Irish language, is *at issue*. The poem presents the definition in dry language, but immediately complicates our attitude to this definition with a more extravagant use of language drawing on a religious semantic field. The poem thereby establishes a pattern of competition between words of markedly different type.

As the poem develops, we realize that the speaker has taken his cue from the name of the place; he wants to suggest that the situation of the flooded village, and the society which has caused this situation, represents 'a hole of the spirit'. Of course, this remains a criticism by implication only – but it is effectively suggested by the careful word-choices. The poem's play of contrasting kinds of language use is perhaps most obvious in the second paragraph. We might think about this in the context of a useful experiment. Often, it is a good idea to cover up parts of a poem, in order to see what it is the words persuade you will come next, what kind of poem it is that the words signal you are reading. Of course, once we move the sheet of paper down the page, we may find that our prediction has not been accurate. The next line may entirely break the spell. If we were to perform a similar experiment with the second paragraph of this example, what kind of poem would we expect it to form part of? I suggest that we might expect a poem so arid and literal that we would not want to read it. We could justify our low expectations by pointing to the deliberately flat sound of 'Shell' (an oil company, after all) and 'hydro-electric works'. So when this kind of language use actually co-exists with the bitter ironies of the fourth paragraph, the relational tension is correspondingly increased.

In that fourth paragraph, the speaker exploits the resonance of the place-names. These names in their original simplicity seem to belong to a very different kind of language use when compared with '*The Shell Guide*'. These are names intended to guide others – they tell us where fields are, after all – but in the context of a world smaller and more intimate than the packaged tourism of '*The Shell Guide*'. Note, too, how the author plays off these monosyllabic names with the more exotic-looking polysyllables of Irish place-names. The speaker parallels our distance from these place-names, our inevitable sense of their strangeness, with our distance from the patterns of community which brought them into being. By the end of the poem, the poet has evoked a kind of drowned language. The emphasis on 'the hole of the spirit' is caught up by different references to the mouth, to bubbles and to blowholes, as though these names which once passed through people's lips are unable to come up for air.

Our final example comes from another Irish poet, Jean Bleakney:

BE CAREFUL OF THE LILIES!

You'd think we'd know by now (Aren't these the days
of cheap Australian wine and huge bouquets?)

that pollen *stains* – not stains so much as sticks
with microscopic barbs. Burnt Orange flecks

indelible as scorch marks. Such a shame
whether it's cashmere or silk or denim.

The starchy buds are so innocuous
at first. Not like that other 'Look at Us!'

brigade. There are too many petals
on chrysanthemums – stiff as funerals.

Carnations are the same – a primped tableau.
It's as if lilies really want to grow

and multiply, the way they purse their lips;
then one by one each pupal bud unzips

to frisky stamens jostling in midair.
They seem to manage this when no one's there

so that, opening the door on a room
askew with incense and lilies in full bloom,

how hard it is not to get intimate;
to resist doing something you might regret

in Burnt Sienna. They're out-and-out chancers,
those lilies, with their fulminant anthers.[3]

Although it relies on characteristics of the English language as it
is spoken in Ireland, Jean Bleakney's poem is altogether lighter than
O'Driscoll's prose-poem. Bleakney's makes much play of idiomatic-sounding

expressions, ones that are loosely framed by everyday conversation, like 'that other "Look at Us!" // brigade' and 'out-and-out chancers'. These are the kind of expressions we could imagine people using in the real world, in normal chat. But the poem also contains word-choices which conspicuously do not belong in everyday conversation, like 'primped tableau' and 'fulminant anthers'. Although we could imagine these formulae appearing in a pretentious garden-centre brochure, we could not imagine anyone using them in normal conversation – without smiling.

The play of diction in this poem loosely matches the display of flowers: they elevate a space, transform dreary environments with splashes of colour. Bleakney catches their transforming power with reference to a specific colour vocabulary: 'Burnt Orange' and 'Burnt Sienna'. But more than this, she captures their ability to 'lift' an environment by herself moving back and forth from a colloquial vocabulary to an elevated one. Of course the ability of flowers to do this is a relational matter – if a room is covered from wall to wall with flowers, then a fresh set of roses will not elevate the space. Bleakney makes a lot of this relative power, comparing the relative appeal of different types of flower. Lilies are made to seem more present to us because Bleakney tells us about the flowers which they are *not* like.

The poem has an appealing intimacy partly because Bleakney uses a range of words which we associate with domestic interiors. Apart from the flowers, there are the references to 'Australian wine', 'cashmere', 'denim', 'door' and 'room'. We associate these words with things which are close to us – objects in a house, people we are speaking to – not such things as, say, 'clouds' and 'mountains' which we generally think of as being 'far away'. This sense of intimacy is appropriate given the poem's frankly sexual undertone. The backdrop of the poem is the power of seduction, and a puzzling over those qualities, illustrated by the lilies, which are likely to seduce us. The sensuality of the vocabulary is one signal of this subtext – we are repeatedly struck by references to things we can smell, see, touch, taste and hear, as well as words with more obvious sexual associations like 'grow' and 'unzip'. The poem maintains this undertone by keeping human presence implicit – we never see any people in the poem, and human beings are implied only by reference to things they wear or use. This accomplishes several things: it makes it easier for us to project ourselves into the poem; it makes the ambiguity more subtle; and it allows the flowers to seem more 'human'. For example, when we read a line like 'to frisky stamens jostling in mid-air', the sensation of movement is marked partly because of the iambic pulse, partly because of a well-chosen, unusual verb, but also because there are no humans moving around in the poem who would make the flowers seem relatively motionless.

Your assignment is to write a poem which brings together words from different contexts, different linguistic registers. You might try, for instance, to have formal-sounding words in one part of the poem and more idiomatic words in another. Or you might try applying words suitable to one context (say, a military operation) to an unusual context (say, a romantic dinner).

Notes

1 Catherine Phillips, ed., *Gerard Manley Hopkins: Selected Poetry* (Oxford: Oxford University Press, 1996), p. 163.
2 Dennis O'Driscoll, *New and Selected Poems* (London: Anvil, 2004), p. 74.
3 Selina Guinness, ed., *The New Irish Poets* (Newcastle: Bloodaxe, 2004), pp. 46–7.

10

Uses of Syntax

Of all the elements which a writer can exploit in a poem, syntax is at once the most powerful and the most neglected. Its neglect is a little puzzling. It may be that some poets think that the subject is too dry and technical, or think that control of it is more properly an accomplishment of prose-writers. It is true that a poet can 'get away' with a limited control of syntax, and make up for that deficiency with energetic imagery or diction or line-breaks, but it seems a pity to leave such a powerful weapon in the locker.

Consider a simple example of the alternative use of subordinate clauses. If I write the sentence *The bomb exploded after we returned from leave and boarded the ship* the message of the sentence will be reasonably clear. You will understand what has happened. But the force of the message will be badly muffled. If I then adjust the sentence so that the main clause – the one which carries the important part of the message – comes last, quite a different effect is achieved: *After we returned from leave and boarded the ship, the bomb exploded.* Not a word of the sentence has been changed, but the emphasis is now focused squarely on the explosion.

One of the most skilful manipulators of syntax was the poet W. B. Yeats. Here is the second section of his great sequence, 'Meditations in Time of Civil War':

MY HOUSE

An ancient bridge, and a more ancient tower,
A farmhouse that is sheltered by its wall,
An acre of stony ground,
Where the symbolic rose can break in flower,

Old ragged elms, old thorns innumerable,
The sound of the rain or sound
Of every wind that blows;
The stilted water-hen
Crossing stream again
Scared by the splashing of a dozen cows;

A winding stair, a chamber arched with stone,
A grey stone fireplace with an open hearth,
A candle and written page.
Il Penseroso's Platonist toiled on
In some like chamber, shadowing forth
How the daemonic rage
Imagined everything.
Benighted travellers
From markets and from fairs
Have seen his midnight candle glimmering.

Two men have founded here. A man-at-arms
Gathered a score of horse and spent his days
In this tumultuous spot,
Where through long wars and sudden night alarms
His dwindling score and he seemed castaways
Forgetting and forgot;
And I, that after me
My bodily heirs may find,
To exalt a lonely mind,
Befitting emblems of adversity.[1]

As a murderous conflict takes place in the countryside around him, Yeats considers how he, as a citizen and non-combatant, stands in relation to it. In particular he ponders this question with reference to the history and atmosphere of the old tower in which he lives. So this part of the poem foregrounds the past within the present, and opposes something static – a house – to something dangerously dynamic – a war. The collision of active and passive in this section reverberates through the syntax. The stanzas have an architectural solidity, a massy monumentalism, which is reflected in the use of verbs. For example, there are no main verbs in the present tense in the poem, indeed there are no main verbs of any tense until the second stanza. The sentences in the first stanza are elliptical – we complete them in our minds with constructs like *Here is [a farmhouse that is sheltered by its wall]* or *I think about [an acre of stony ground]*. By dropping the main verbs, Yeats gives the reader a sense of action which is taking place, or which has already taken place, elsewhere. This is quite appropriate for a poem partly about a conflict not taking place in the speaker's immediate presence. It is also appropriate for a poem about a structure which has been built long ago, for the building is itself a record of the actions of those who planned and built it.

Another effect of removing the main verbs is to make the house seem unoccupied – or at best occupied only by the ghostly presence of the speaker. The implied subject of these sentences is the author who is viewing, or thinking about, his own house, but this is not mentioned until almost the very end of the section. Therefore all this viewing of, and thinking about, the house is an activity distributed to others – to the reader and to the previous occupants. We might say that Yeats, as he recedes syntactically from the opening stanzas, gives up a little bit of ownership, of the imaginative ownership at any rate, of the house. A further effect of this is to make the house itself seem more substantial, more of a personality, even as its occupants and spectators recede.

Like the first stanza, the second opens in a similar vein. The reader does not encounter a main verb until the reference to '*Il Penseroso*'s Platonist'. Yeats wants to identify with the subject-matter of Milton's poem and so he grants the first main verb, 'toiled', to a figure in that poem. The effect is to make a fictional figure from a seventeenth-century poem appear more present and more active than the real human beings in the present (especially those who are fighting a war outside).

One other syntactical figure we might note is the contrasting use of sentence-types in the final stanza. The almost throwaway first sentence is so short and colourless that one is tempted to pass over it quickly without registering that it acts as a set-up for the much longer, but syntactically less complete, concluding sentence. When reading the first sentence, we do not immediately recognize that Yeats is numbering himself among the 'two men' – indeed, we do not realize this until near the conclusion of the last stanza. The purpose again seems to be let him distance himself from the active forces in the poem. The long sentence seems to place him in a line – the syntax connects him, as he wants to be connected, to a functioning line of people who have occupied the house – as though the house were looking after him rather than the other way around. Notice the way the 'I' which represents Yeats is not paired with a main verb. The 'I' serves mainly to introduce a further line of occupiers who are coming after him. Whether or not all this syntactical modesty on Yeats's part is calculated or genuine, the effects are consistent and powerful.

Here is an example taken from the work of a later Irish poet, Michael Longley:

PHOENIX

I'll hand to you six duck eggs Orla Murphy gave me
In a beechwood bowl Ted O'Driscoll turned, a nest
Jiggling eggs from Baltimore to Belfast, from friends
You haven't met, a double-yolk inside each shell
Laid by a duck that renovates and begets itself
Inside my head as the phoenix, without grass or corn,
On a strict diet of frankincense and cardamoms,
After five centuries builds with talon and clean beak
In the top branches of a quivering palm his nest,
Lining it with cassia, spikes of nard, cinnamon chips
And yellow myrrh, brooding among the spicy smells
His own death and giving birth to an only child
Who grows up to carry through thin air the heavy nest
– His cradle, his father's coffin – to the sun's city,
In front of the sun's doorway putting his bundle down
As I shall put down the eggs Orla Murphy gave me
In a beechwood bowl Ted O'Driscoll turned for her.[2]

In 'Phoenix', we find syntax used in an evidently self-conscious way in the form of a one-sentence poem. Longley specializes in this form and there are many examples of it in his work. The value of bringing together all the poem's elements within a single sentence is that they become functionally connected. As readers try to make sense of the sentence, as a grammatical entity, they naturally allow the various elements to colour one another. The disadvantage of this strategy is that the sentence, by virtue of its length, may seem confused and unwieldy.

Unlike Yeats in the example above, Longley does not suppress the main verb of his sentence. But he does treat it in an unusual way – collapsing it into the idiomatic 'I'll'. In effect the main verb, on which the rest of the poem hinges, has flashed past us before we can fully register its presence and significance. Reading this line for the first time, we don't know how long the sentence is going to be, so the effect is one of having been hood-winked by the unassuming opening. The use of the future tense is also strange, because it turns out to encompass events which look hard to predict. It takes in, for example, some ordinary realistic events (like the gift of some duck eggs) as well as some events which take place in the speaker's imag-ination (like the birth of a phoenix). The speaker is as certain about the simple gift as he is about the imagined, or to-be-imagined, event, and the emotional register of that syntactic situation – how odd that he should feel this way about the future – gives the poem an important tug. Because the main verb comes at the start, the rest of the poem presents us with a series of subordinate clauses. Longley controls the potential confusion of these clauses by presenting us with a series of circular motifs: some eggs, a bowl, a nest, the prominents 'o's of 'O'Driscoll' and 'Orla', and the circular live-die cycle of the phoenix. Note the small switch from 'I'll' to the more for-mal-sounding 'I shall' – it is not a complete syntactic return, but it is close enough to impress on the reader that the poem has a circular structure. Longley wants to suggest that acts of the imagination are collaborative – they depend on others like 'Orla Murphy' and 'Ted O'Driscoll' – in the way that parts of a sentence collaborate to influence the reader's mind.

The poet Robert Frost thought of sentences as the basic unit of poetry, and emphasized the importance of how sentences are performed in actual speech. Frost's theory focused on the way meaning is suggested by the move-ment of sentences independent of the words used. By way of illustration, he invites us to imagine overhearing a conversation which is taking place behind a shut door. The door cuts off the words but not the rhythm and flow of the conversation. That rhythm and flow will seem to convey a mean-ing, or more likely meanings, of their own. Indeed, as we all know, the rhythm and flow of someone's speech can convey something directly opposite to the words being used, something different to how it would look if you wrote it down. In his study of Frost's poetry, Richard Poirier traces Frost's con-cept directly back to William James, to a chapter in James's *The Principles of Psychology* called 'The Stream of Thought' (a phrase which would partly inspire the phrase 'stream-of-consciousness'). In that chapter, James says: 'The truth is that large tracts of human speech are nothing but signs of direction in thought, of which direction we nevertheless have an acutely discriminative sense, though no definite sensorial image plays any part in it whatsoever.'[3]

We find a good example of these 'signs of direction in thought' in the syntax of Robert Frost's poem 'Come In':

COME IN

As I came to the edge of the woods,
Thrush music – hark!
Now if it was dusk outside,
Inside it was dark.

Too dark in the woods for a bird
By sleight of wing
To better its perch for the night,
Though it still could sing.

The last of the light of the sun
That had died in the west
Still lived for one song more
In a thrush's breast.

Far in the pillared dark
Thrush music went –
Almost like a call to come in
To the dark and lament.

But no, I was out for stars:
I would not come in.
I meant not even if asked,
And I hadn't been.[4]

The poem turns very much on its final stanza, in which the sentence sounds sharply alter. As I read the poem, the speaker and the thrush represent two different kinds of voice. While the thrush is rhetorical and overdramatic, the speaker favours a more subtle kind of music/speaking/ poetry. For a while, the speaker is tempted to join the bird – indeed the speaker toys with this idea up to the final stanza. We might think of the speaker as pondering the value of writing a kind of poetry worthy of the nineteenth century (mainly represented by the voice of the bird). Hints of this are provided by the old-fashioned exclamation 'hark', the over-the-top image of the sun dying in the west, and the syntax of the early stanzas.

Stanza 2, for example, uses ellipsis, dropping the main verb, an effect which at first sight seems colloquial. But the second line does not sound colloquial at all (the phrase, 'sleight of wing', is too careful and sly) and

105

this, retrospectively, makes the first line seem stilted. Stanza 4 also sounds 'poetic' in a noticeable way. It begins with an old-fashioned looking inversion which immediately heightens the language – compare the effect of the normal word-order: thrush music went / far in the pillared dark.

At the point where the poem turns away from the thrush's rhetoric, the sentence sounds decisively change. Most immediately we notice how the last stanza reintroduces the personal pronoun – this functions as a clear signal of self-possession and self-assertion – the pronoun 'I' is voiced in every single line. We can imagine how this would sound in a conversation, at the end, perhaps, of a long story. Having suppressed the pronoun for so long, the speaker suddenly over-uses the word in order to send out a tonal signal. In the language of William James, we see the signs of the speaker's thought taking another direction. The last two lines ring a very identifiable sentence-sound. The speaker dispenses with inversion and ellipsis, preferring sentences with normal word-order. Although these sentences are grammatically simple, they contain a colloquial undercurrent. The sound that they make is that of someone who knows that there is an issue at stake (whether or not the speaker has been invited into the woods) and who knows that the listener knows this too. Only in the last line, which has the snap of any good punch-line, does the speaker signal to the listener that he has been aware of this issue all along, that it has not passed him by. As Frost said in another context, only somebody who has heard sentences in action, who has heard language performed in complicated emotional situations, will pick up on a sound like this. The subtlety of the sound from these concluding sentences is in decisive contrast to the received rhetoric of the opening stanzas. Frost demonstrates that sentence-structure has its own charm and colour – the shape of a sentence carries its own range of association every bit as much as a word or a phrase.

Your assignment is to write a poem which makes deliberate use of syntax. You might, for example, choose to write (1) a poem without any verbs, (2) a poem which suppresses its syntactic subject, (3) a poem in which the tense of the verbs changes in the final stanza, or (4) a poem which is a single sentence.

Notes

1   W. B. Yeats, *The Collected Poems of W. B. Yeats*, 1st edn. 1933, 2nd edn. 1950 (London: Macmillan, 1982), pp. 226–7.
2   Michael Longley, *Selected Poems* (London: Jonathan Cape, 1998), p. 115.
3   William James, *The Principles of Psychology*, vol. 1, general ed. Frederick H. Burkhardt, textual ed. Fredson Bowers, associate ed. Ignas K. Skrupskelis (Cambridge, MA: Harvard University Press, 1981), p. 233.
4   Edward Connery Latham, ed., *The Poetry of Robert Frost* (New York: Henry Holt, 1979), p. 334.

11

Tone

Human beings are good at saying one thing and meaning another. Sometimes we use tone to signal another meaning to a listener, sometimes we use tone to signal another meaning to ourselves. Even a simple expression like 'It is a nice day' can be asked to convey any number of messages from 'It is not a nice day' to 'I am so happy' to 'I am really miserable'. Some contemporary poems are guilty of using a relatively narrow range of tones. Robert Frost once wrote, with an air of understated dismissiveness, how the poets of his time were apt to exclaim using only one tone, that of 'O soul!' or 'O hills!' As he pointed out, the conversational *ah*, *oh* or *uh* can, in tonal terms, contain multitudes – and a skilful poet should be able to exploit such possibilities. At poetry readings, one sometimes hears poems delivered in tones of hushed solemnity, as though they formed part of a sacred ritual. While there may be a right tone for a TV anchor at a state funeral, it is fatal to think that there is a right tone for delivering poetry. In poetry, no tone is more or less appropriate. Indeed as the poems in this chapter by Wislawa Szymborska and Elizabeth Bishop show, many of the best effects are achieved by poets who are willing to exploit a wide tonal range.

To start with a small example, consider Anne Carson's version of a poem by Catullus. Only a poet with a love for quirky conversational tones could arrive at the surprise of the last line:

QUINTIA FORMOSAST MULTIS (QUINTIA IS BEAUTIFUL TO MANY)

Catullus compares a certain Quintia to his own love.

There was a whiteness in you.
That kitten washed in another world look.
Good strong handshake for a girl but.
But.[1]

Whereas the second line is almost too beautiful, the last line brings us to earth with a firm bump. Carson has captured a special tone which we know from conversation but which we may never have seen deployed in a poetic setting. Unless we are impressed by this capture, the poem may strike us as worryingly slight. But I think this poem has a fresh quality because it gives us the informal feel of a mind in motion, of somebody thinking on the spot. We can almost see the speaker weighing up what he wants to say and, when coming to a decisive conclusion, finding pathos and humour in this discovery.

Indeed, tone is an excellent vehicle for humour – and it is rare to find a poet with a wide tonal range who is not also good-humoured. Frequently, tone is used in parodic poems, which generally rely on the reader knowing the voice which is being lampooned. Consider 'Henry King' by Hilaire Belloc. The poem aims to parody the kind of instructive poems for children which were popular in Victorian times. Belloc parodies the pomposity of such verse with cutting effect:

HENRY KING

Who chewed bits of String, and was early cut off in Dreadful Agonies

The Chief Defect of Henry King
Was chewing little bits of String.
At last he swallowed some which tied
Itself in ugly Knots inside.
Physicians of the Utmost Fame
Were called at once; but when they came
They answered, as they took their Fees,
'There is no Cure for this Disease.
Henry will very soon be dead.'
His Parents stood about his Bed

109

> Lamenting his Untimely Death,
> When Henry, with his Latest Breath,
> Cried – 'Oh, my Friends, be warned by me,
> That Breakfast, Dinner, Lunch, and Tea
> Are all the Human Frame requires . . .'
> With that the Wretched Child expires.[2]

Belloc's parody depends on so exaggerating the dreadful circumstances of this child that the various tones become comically inappropriate. The poem is in its own way very unsentimental (itself unusual in any poem about children) – with the kind of sardonicism and sarcasm which we are more likely to associate with cynical adult wit. Belloc parodies the pompous tone of authority from the very first line – 'chief defect' is a phrase almost unimaginable from a parent who is talking about their child – and this roundabout, constipated phrase is echoed by the solemn way in which the child's full name is used (imagine the difference if the first line read 'The trouble with Henry': we would not be alerted to expect something off-key). The solemnity of the opening is rendered instantly ludicrous by the next line when we learn what is the matter. We might say that in the second line the poem displays its 'undertone', a sly knowingness which winks at the reader, indicating that all of this is a bit of grotesque fun. The two pieces of reported speech contrast humorously with the tone of the poem's speaker. The cynical-sounding doctors seem to be more interested in their fees than in the welfare of the child, while Henry's exclamation at the end sounds absurdly moralistic. The reader registers that this is just the kind of over-obliging remark that we might expect in a Victorian poem – whose upshot is merely that the child should eat regular meals.

Although the next two poems depend heavily on tone, they are different in many respects. Dwelling on a variety of speakers, Wislawa Szymborska's poem picks up the kinds of tone we use when we are at a public occasion in the company of people we know. Elizabeth Bishop's poem, by contrast, has only one speaker, and inhabits the kind of 'inward tone' we use when we are thinking to ourselves. Here is Szymborska's poem, which plays with the voices heard at a funeral (incidentally, it is also a good example of polyphony):

FUNERAL

'so suddenly, who could have seen it coming'
'stress and smoking, I kept telling him'

'not bad, thanks, and you'
'these flowers need to be unwrapped'
'his brother's heart gave out, too, it runs in the family'
'I'd never know you in that beard'
'he was asking for it, always mixed up in something'
'that new guy was going to make a speech, I don't see him'
'Kazek's in Warsaw, Tadek has gone abroad'
'you were smart, you brought the only umbrella'
'so what if he was more talented than they were'
'no, it's a walk-through room, Barbara won't take it'
'of course, he was right, but that's no excuse'
'with body work and paint, just guess how much'
'two egg yolks and a tablespoon of sugar'
'none of his business, what was in it for him'
'only in blue and just small sizes'
'five times and never any answer'
'all right, so I could have, but you could have, too'
'good thing that at least she still had a job'
'don't know, relatives, I guess'
'that priest looks just like Belmondo'
'I've never been in this part of the grounds'
'I dreamed about him last night, I had a feeling'
'his daughter's not bad-looking'
'the way of all flesh'
'give my best to the widow, I've got to run'
'it all sounded so much more solemn in Latin'
'what's gone is gone'
'goodbye'
'I could sure use a drink'
'give me a call'
'which bus goes downtown'
'I'm going this way'
'we're not'[3]

Given the solemn setting, Szymborska's poem achieves a startling range by including snatches of conversation we might not think best suited to the occasion. These range from the serious and wistful to the banal and pompous. The different kinds of voice allow us to experience, at one remove, the different kinds of people at the funeral. All we hear are voices and yet the poem successfully gives the impression that all human life is present.

Obviously such uncoordinated variety has its pitfalls. Szymborska needs to give the voices a certain amount of play, let them be natural and believable, without making the poem seem random. Another consideration is that the voices must not bore us (in the way that conversations overheard sometimes do). Szymborska meets these demands with an artful use of contrast. She separates the more serious tones of voice – the ones we might expect in this context – and places between them the more casual-sounding remarks. The reader can see what might be lost, for example, if the line 'so what if he was more talented than they were' were set down beside the line 'none of his business, what was in it for him'. Since both these phrases sound tetchy and exasperated, the surprise of contrast would disappear. Although the poem is quite different from 'Henry King', in one important respect they are the same. Both poems use death as a backdrop. Because of that we judge the various voices in relation to that unavoidable context. So flippant remarks like 'that priest looks just like Belmondo' are coloured by the funeral setting. The reader thinks, *hang on, here is someone who makes jokes at funerals*. If the occasion of the poem were more casual – say, the record of voices heard in a café – then it would be impossible to colour remarks in this fashion. The relationship between the tone and the context is critical. By choosing to set the poem at a funeral, Szymborska gives to her voices a common interest, a shared point of reference, which gives more bite to their varied responses.

At the beginning of the poem, we are not sure if we are reading the transcript of one conversation or many. We might, for instance, imagine lines one and two as being spoken by a pair in conversation, and assume that this conversation continued through the rest of the poem. Only gradually do we realize that this is not so. A major clue is provided by the transition from the solemnity of line 5 to the glibness of 'I'd never know you in that beard'. Szymborska also gives us a sense of time passing – the briefer remarks are made at the end when the participants are tired, no longer able to expend the energy of sociability. The ending acutely captures the desire of people, exhausted from seeing old friends and acquaintances and unwelcomely conscious of their own mortality, to escape back into their own lives. In that brilliant final line, we hear the snap of tiredness, a voice reaching its limit with the company of another.

We find a much more lonely-sounding voice in 'Five Flights Up' by Elizabeth Bishop:

FIVE FLIGHTS UP

Still dark.
The unknown bird sits on his usual branch.

The little dog next door barks in his sleep
inquiringly, just once.
Perhaps in his sleep, too, the bird inquires
once or twice, quavering.
Questions – if that is what they are –
answered directly, simply,
by day itself.

Enormous morning, ponderous, meticulous;
gray light streaking each bare branch,
each single twig, along one side,
making another tree, of glassy veins . . .
The bird still sits there. Now he seems to yawn.

The little black dog runs in his yard.
His owner's voice arises, stern,
'You ought to be ashamed!'
What has he done?
He bounces cheerfully up and down;
he rushes in circles in the fallen leaves.

Obviously, he has no sense of shame.
He and the bird know everything is answered,
all taken care of,
no need to ask again.
– Yesterday brought to today so lightly!
(A yesterday I find almost impossible to lift.)[4]

By contrast with that of 'Henry King', the speaker's voice here is quite understated. Indeed, so understated is the poem as a whole that its subtleties might altogether elude us. Bishop establishes a casual, thoughtful tone with the use of simple colloquial sentences like 'The little black dog runs in his yard' – it could almost be a child speaking. As it slowly follows the onset of morning, the voice is noticeably tired. Right through the poem we have the sense of a person who is finding it hard to think, and the tone of voice we hear is one we might associate with depression. From the very first line, we have a sense of effort, of moving almost reluctantly over the line-break. The phrase 'Still dark' is a colloquial way of saying that it is not yet morning, but it also has a secondary sense of the outlook being dark. Bishop accentuates this sombre tone by ensuring that a lot of sentences coincide with a single line. Because the line-length is irregular, the poem seems reluctant to get going – it never establishes a consistent rhythm.

113

The one voice that does stick out in the poem is the overheard shout of Bishop's neighbour. This agitated exclamation is entirely out of keeping with the slow pace of the poem and yet it seems to resonate with the speaker. Bishop's brooding tone is a sign that this question (of what the dog needs to be ashamed about) has struck home, as if it bears obscurely on herself. The poem brilliantly captures this inward voice of brooding, the sense of the mind's wheel grinding away at trifles, the kind of self-questioning which results from some kind of trauma. At the end of the poem, we are told – reluctantly – that something has happened yesterday to hurt the speaker. What is at first puzzling about the poem is that it does not name the problem, does not make it obvious that the tone she is using has been caused by some external pressure. What makes the poem more painful is the contrast between the unworried animals and the speaker. The creatures of the natural world are able to treat the morning as a new start, are naturally untroubled by their own 'questions'. Bishop is left to envy a serenity she cannot share. 'Five Flights Up' is unusual. Most poems of unhappiness are more explicitly about the writer's trouble. Through her use of tone, Bishop has found a way to explore personal misery, which is refreshingly directed towards things outside the self.

Your assignment is to write a poem with a variety of tones. You might do this by having a variety of speakers, or by having a single speaker who has mixed feelings on a subject, or who is speaking at different times. Pay special attention to the way in which one tone changes to another, for it is through such transitions that tone most effects the reader.

Notes

1   Anne Carson, *Men in the Off Hours* (New York: Knopf, 2000), p. 43.
2   Hilaire Belloc, *Selected Cautionary Verse*, 1st edn. 1940 (Harmondsworth: Penguin, 1958), pp. 20–3.
3   Wislawa Szymborska, *View with a Grain of Sand: Selected Poems* (London: Harvest, 1995), pp. 157–8.
4   Elizabeth Bishop, *Complete Poems* (London: Chatto, 1991), p. 181.

12

Traditional Forms: Ode

Sometimes we view a traditional form in the way we may view poetry, like a uniform into which we must squeeze, adjusting ourselves to the structure rather than the other way around. But however old a traditional form may be, it is not unalterable. When we survey their history we find that every traditional form has been tweaked and developed, indeed that every form is no more than the sum of its adjustments. We learn that if a form is to live, its adjustment is not just a possibility, it is a necessity. As my introduction makes clear, I prefer to steer away from those forms – sonnet, sestina, villanelle – which are usually offered in books of this sort. As an alternative, I have selected two traditional forms, the ode and the epistle, which I will look at in this chapter and the next.

For the purposes of this chapter, I define an ode as a poem of praise on a public subject. However, this is not the only possible definition. The form has a long history, and consequently there many different models which one might follow. For example, you may find the ode defined elsewhere as a poem written on a public subject in an elevated manner. There were two original models of the ode, one Greek (generally associated with Pindar) and one Roman (generally associated with Horace). Based on the choral songs from Greek drama, Pindar's odes had a markedly public quality. Some were written to praise athletes at the Olympic Games. The Horatian tradition tends to be more meditative and it is in this tradition that we place the well-known odes of Keats. When taken up by English poets, the form was extended to poems in praise of every conceivable thing – from living creatures and inanimate objects to abstract concepts.

It is unfortunate that many modern poems are chronically turned in upon themselves, morbid and solemn almost by default. Thanks to its history,

115

the ode is a form which encourages the writer to turn their gaze outward. As the poet C. D. Wright has written, '[an] ode is given to improving on things as they are actually to be found'. It encourages an attitude of praise. It also uses a complex form of address. Since the poet is usually praising someone or something which cannot 'answer back', the question naturally arises: 'To what degree is the apparent addressee of the ode the actual addressee?' The ode admits a complex tone of address. Because of its public orientation, it can be a little hard for the ode to deal with private, personal experience in a comfortable way. Whatever private matter the poet wants to explore in this form, they will feel a pressure to relate it to others in an accessible fashion. An ode is not a good place for opacity of thought or obscurity of feeling. Nor is it a good place for bringing together fragments of observation, or half-formed thoughts. An ode works better when it transmits a finished, considered point of view, in the manner of a lively, persuasive essay.

Here is one example of the use to which English poets put the ode in the eighteenth century. The poem is 'Ode to Evening' by William Collins:

ODE TO EVENING

If aught of oaten stop or pastoral song
May hope, chaste Eve, to soothe thy modest ear,
   Like thy own solemn springs,
   Thy springs, and dying gales,
O nymph reserved, while now the bright-haired sun
Sits in yon western tent, whose cloudy skirts,
   With brede ethereal wove,
   O'erhang his wavy bed;

Now air is hushed, save where the weak-eyed bat
With short shrill shriek flits by on leathern wing,
   Or where the beetle winds
   His small but sullen horn,
As oft he rises 'midst the twilight path,
Against the pilgrim borne in heedless hum:
   Now teach me, maid composed,
   To breathe some softened strain,
Whose numbers stealing through thy darkening vale
May not unseemly with its stillness suit,
   As, musing slow, I hail
   Thy genial loved return!

For when thy folding star arising shows
His paly circlet, at his warning lamp
   The fragrant hours, and elves
   Who slept in buds the day,
And many a nymph who wreathes her brows with sedge
And sheds the freshening dew, and lovelier still,
   The Pensive Pleasures sweet,
   Prepare thy shadowy car.

Then lead, calm votaress, where some sheety lake
Cheers the lone heath, or some time-hallowed pile,
   Or upland fallows grey,
   Reflect its last cool gleam.
Or if chill blustering winds or driving rain
Forbid my willing feet, be mine the hut
   That from the mountain's side
   Views wilds and swelling floods,
And hamlets brown, and dim-discovered spires,
And hears their simple bell, and marks o'er all
   Thy dewy fingers draw
   The gradual dusky veil.

While Spring shall pour his showers, as oft he wont,
And bathe thy breathing tresses, meekest Eve!
   While Summer loves to sport
   Beneath thy lingering light;
While sallow Autumn fills thy lap with leaves,
Or Winter, yelling through the troublous air,
   Affrights thy shrinking train,
   And rudely rends thy robes;
So long, sure-found beneath the sylvan shed,
Shall Fancy, Friendship, Science, rose-lipped Health,
   Thy gentlest influence own,
   And hymn thy favourite name![1]

This is a reflective poem. The poet explores a mood which in another form might easily lapse into self-absorption. The speaker is not in search of human company and yet there is a kind of sociable loneliness in the poem. While not all addresses to the external world are positive, the direction which the ode faces – unambiguously outwards towards the world – is in itself positive. Collins is not bound to say anything nice about the evening, but the guiding assumption of the form encourages his praise. It is noticeable that from the beginning of the poem our attention is turned on the personified figure of evening, 'Eve', and that the speaker does not refer to himself until the fifteenth line. The emphasis falls on '*thy* modest ear', '*thy* darkening vale'.

Collins invokes the totality of evening with a deft shift of scales. We move from the wide-angled sunset of the first stanza to the lovely detail of the beetle's 'sullen horn' in the second. No aspect of evening is too great or small for Collins's praise. Indeed so complete is Collins's celebration that it shades into a kind of ecstatic submission. Whereas the bulk of contemporary poems weaken the external world in order to embrace subjectivity, Collins does the opposite. His speaker effaces himself to the point of erasure. Note how much of the poem refers to 'Eve', and to evening in general, in terms of clothing: 'robes', 'veil', 'skirts', a wreath of 'sedge'. Taken together with the images of the hut, the 'folding star', and the elves that sleep in flowers, we see that the poem dwells on motifs of enclosure. The poet wants to be folded in the clothes of evening so completely that he will lose his identity.

Collins draws this lengthy meditation together through a combination of leisurely syntax and careful sonic patterning. The first line signals the speed and sound of what is to come with a mixture of long vowels and labials. Note the way that the first two stressed syllables ('If *aught* of *oaten*') coincide with the first two long vowel-sounds and how these are echoed in the 'o-sounds' that follow. The first sentence is lazily draped over the whole of the first two stanzas. By opening with subordinate clauses, the poet signals that he has plenty of time for his address – the main clause can wait till the fifteenth line. Notice how a much later line like 'While Spring shall pour his showers, as oft he wont' picks up many of the sounds we hear in the first line. Given that the poet has invoked melody from the start, the emphasis on sonic patterning is appropriate – the poem becomes a kind of extended song.

If the subject of Collins's ode seems abstract, then that of Szymborska's next poem is definitively so:

PI

The admirable number pi:
three point one four one.
All the following digits are also initial,
five nine two because it never ends.

It can't be comprehended *six five three five* at a glance,
eight nine by calculation,
seven nine or imagination,
not even *three two three eight* by wit, that is, by comparison
four six to anything else
two six four three in the world.
The longest snake on earth calls it quits at about forty feet.
Likewise, snakes of myth and legend, though they may hold out a bit longer.
The pageant of digits comprising the number pi
doesn't stop at the page's edge.
It goes on across the table, through the air,
over a wall, a leaf, a bird's nest, clouds, straight into the sky,
through all the bottomless, bloated heavens.
Oh how brief – a mouse tail, a pigtail – is the tail of a comet!
How feeble the star's ray, bent by bumping up against space!
While here we have *two three fifteen three hundred nineteen*
my phone number your shirt size the year
nineteen hundred and seventy-three the sixth floor
the number of inhabitants sixty-five cents
hip measurement two fingers a charade, a code,
in which we find *hail to thee, blithe spirit, bird thou never wert*
alongside *ladies and gentlemen, no cause for alarm,*
as well as *heaven and earth shall pass away,*
but not the number pi, oh no, nothing doing,
it keeps right on with its rather remarkable *five,*
its uncommonly fine *eight,*
its far from final *seven,*
nudging, always nudging a sluggish eternity
to continue.[2]

Szymborska's poem tackles a subject which at first sight does not look very promising. How does one write a poem about the number *pi*? It is even more difficult to imagine how to accomplish this if you believe that all poems have to contain material which is obviously personal. This is not a poem which arises, spontaneously, from events in the author's life, or which reflects moments of unusually intense feeling. Instead, Szymborska has elected to tackle a subject rather as a newspaper columnist might, a publicly available topic of no special urgency, the kind of poem which anyone might choose to write.

There is a democratic quality to this kind of poem – for it does not seem to mark out an audience for itself – it is not a poem meant exclusively for highbrows, or the young, or some minority group – it is a poem for anyone who has heard of the number pi. An advantage of the ode – a poem on a public topic – is that an author can write one at any time about almost anything – the audience does not assume that the writer of the ode has been through a special emotional experience, as one might assume if one were reading a confessional poem. The poet needs no special 'permission' or validation to write it.

Although it is a poem of an idiosyncratic personality, one can tell that 'Pi' is not a poem about a peculiar personal experience. In part this is because of the way in which Szymborska uses the pronoun 'we'. In using this word, there is an assumption that the speaker is pointing towards thoughts and feelings which are widely shared. She envisions a humanity on whose part it is possible to speak, a good example of a persuasive use of address. What is also notable about the subject-matter of the poem is that Szymborksa is celebrating something – is it a thing? – which has qualities that make it seem inhuman. That is to say, this is a democratic poem about something which is very undemocratic. Much of the effect of the poem is generated by playing off the eternal with the mortal – pi goes on forever, human beings do not. As Szymborska figures it, the number pi can pass through, and beyond all of our merely temporary human arrangements, from ordinary combinations of numbers to extraordinary combinations of words. Viewed from a certain perspective, then, the reader might wonder what it is that Szymborksa thinks 'admirable' about this number, since its abstract immortality contrasts so sharply with our obvious mortality. At another level, though, we can read the existence of pi as reassuring, for it, like the concept of eternity, is a human creation, a testament to the power of the human imagination. At the end of the poem, Szymborska finds another strong reason to admire the number in the fact that it continues. Ironically, this is where the poem stops – a place of uneasy rest as we imagine the number pi extending beyond the bounds of the poem.

Our final example is of an ode, written by Frank O'Hara, which is self-consciously celebratory, indeed, almost evangelical about the quality of its excitement:

ODE TO JOY

We shall have everything we want and there'll be no more dying
   on the pretty plains or in the supper clubs
for our symbol we'll acknowledge vulgar materialistic laughter
   over an insatiable sexual appetite

and the streets will be filled with racing forms
and the photographs of murderers and narcissists and movie-stars
   will swell from the walls and books alive in steaming rooms
   to press against our burning flesh not once but interminably
as water flows down hill into the full-lipped basin
and the adder dives for the ultimate ostrich egg
and the feather cushion preens beneath a reclining monolith
   that's sweating with post-exertion visibility and sweetness
   near the grave of love

                    No more dying

We shall see the grave of love as a lovely sight and temporary
   near the elm that spells the lovers' names in roots
and there'll be no more music but the ears in lips and no more wit
   but tongues in ears and no more drums but ears to thighs
as evening signals nudities unknown to ancestors' imaginations
and the imagination itself will stagger like a tired paramour of ivory
   under the sculptural necessities of lust that never falters
   like a six-mile runner from Sweden or Liberia covered with gold
as lava flows up and over the far-down somnolent city's abdication
and the hermit always wanting to be lone is lone at last
and the weight of external heat crushes the heat-hating Puritan
   who's self-defeating vice becomes a proper sepulchre at last
   that love may live

Buildings will go up into the dizzy air as love itself goes in
   and up the reeling life that it has chosen for once or all
while in the sky a feeling of intemperate fondness will excite the birds
   to swoop and veer like flies crawling across absorbed limbs
that weep a pearly perspiration on the sheets of brief attention
and the hairs dry out that summon anxious declaration of the organs
   as they rise like buildings to the needs of temporary neighbours
   pouring hunger through the heart to feed desire in intravenous ways
like the ways of gods with humans in the innocent combination of light
and flesh or as the legends ride with their heroes through the dark to found
great cities where all life is possible to maintain as long as time
   which wants us to remain for cocktails in a bar and after dinner
   lets us live with it

                    No more dying[3]

121

On one level, this is a very simple poem, which amply illustrates the power of celebration. While some elements of the poem's imagery are not straightforward, the overall thrust of the poem is one of breathless excitement. O'Hara is one of the few poets who can use an enthusiastic tone convincingly, and the ode is a form he uses on many occasions. The poem's breathlessness owes much to its lack of punctuation. There is nothing to stop the reader being propelled along from one image to another, and the longish lines only reinforce this plunging effect. O'Hara's poem is not only a matter of praise. Each stanza is a single sentence, a pattern only slightly interrupted by the brief wish for 'No more dying'. So while the overall tone is one of praise, there are some quiet undercurrents in the verse as well. Looked at more closely, aspects of the 'joyful' behaviour which O'Hara calls for are a little troubling. Why does he want the photographs of 'murderers and narcissists and movie-stars' to press against our 'burning flesh'? Is this really something which we should look forward to? Should we want our imaginations to approximate a 'tired paramour of ivory'?

In effect, the poem is a moral embrace of amoral behaviour. It is a poem which has no time for cautious principles or circumspect advice. Rather than celebrating the images it flashes up, what the poem really celebrates is what those images do. They may be disturbing, but they are all exciting, and it is this capacity to feel excited which more than anything else interests the poem. O'Hara celebrates the vigour of imagining 'a six-mile runner from Sweden or Liberia covered with gold' and an adder diving 'for the ultimate ostrich egg'. It is the power of these images which really matters. A sunny day and a Sunday morning stroll, for instance, might be things which make us happy, but how colourless and limp such examples would be compared with O'Hara's fizzing imagery. What the poem shows is the power of the ode to transform its material with happiness, even when that material incorporates many negative-seeming things which surround us. And it is 'us'. Unlike the self-absorbed happiness typical of children, what O'Hara wants is for others to be happy too, and this leads the poem's speaker to recommend a general release from spiritual bondage. O'Hara's enthusiasm is good for him and, just as importantly, may be good for us.

Your assignment is to write an ode. Whether fervent or mild, your tone should be one of praise. Try to direct your praise towards someone or something off the beaten track – you might, for example, write an ode to credit cards or to laziness. Above all, allow the mode of praise to draw out feelings for things which you might not be expected to have.

Notes

1   Helen Gardner, ed., *The New Oxford Book of English Verse 1250–1950* (Oxford: Clarendon Press, 1972), pp. 452–3.
2   Wislawa Szymborska, *View with a Grain of Sand: Selected Poems* (London: Harvest, 1995), pp. 129–30.
3   Donald Merriarn Allen, ed., *The Collected Poems of Frank O'Hara* (New York: Knopf, 1971), p. 281.

13

Traditional Forms: Epistle

Like the ode, the epistle has a long history and is a relatively flexible form. In Latin literature, the principle writer of epistles was Horace, who used the verse-letter to address occasional subjects in an essay-like style. The form was widespread in eighteenth-century England, where Alexander Pope did much to popularize it. The particular form associated with Pope, decasyllabic rhyming couplets, continues to influence verse-letters. In general, verse-letters adopt a regular, formal, rhyming style. In modern times, the revival of the epistle was mainly due to W. H. Auden – his 'Letter to Lord Byron' explored a flexible, chatty form, 'large enough to swim in', which could move quickly across subjects trivial and serious.

The verse-letter discourages pretension – in this form the writer is usually addressing somebody with whom they feel they are on equal terms. And it is a form in which the writer does not have to pretend to be a god-like visionary. The poet may mention (as Auden mentions in 'Letter to Lord Byron') that they have a cold, or that they are writing on a bus. Verse-letters can include material which it is hard to include in other styles: recipes, jokes, puns, gossip. Often they draw attention to the moment of their composition (in an example below, W. S. Graham's lines 'I am up. I've washed / The front of my face'), a motif which can be used for humorous and dramatic effects. Rarely is the tone of a verse-letter one of high seriousness – indeed the form seems to work best when there is a noticeably wide variation of tone.

Verse-letters usually emphasize the social sphere. Since friendship is (naturally enough) one of the form's major preoccupations, a verse-letter will often revolve around the social mores of a particular group. A poet often turns to this form when they cannot find another way to draw together highly diverse subject-matter. Sometimes the poem will draw attention to its rather ramshackle, provisional construction and, in general, this unbuttoned style humanizes the speaker.

Here is an example of a verse-letter by one Irish poet, Michael Longley, to another:

LETTER TO SEAMUS HEANEY

From Carrigskeewaun in Killadoon
I write, although I'll see you soon,
Hoping this fortnight detonates
Your year in the United States,
Offering you by way of welcome
To the sick counties we call home
The mystical point at which I tire
Of Calor gas and a turf fire.

Till we talk again in Belfast
Pleasanter far to leave the past
Across three acres and two brooks
On holiday in a post box
Which dripping fuchsia bells surround,
Its back to the prevailing wind,
And where sanderlings from Iceland
Court the breakers, take my stand,

Disinfecting with a purer air
That small subconscious cottage where
The Irish poet slams his door
On slow-worm, toad and adder:
Beneath these racing skies it is
A tempting stance indeed – *ipsis*
Hibernicis hibernicores –
Except that we know the old stories,

The midden of cracked hurley sticks
Tied to recall the crucifix,
Of broken bones and lost scruples,
The blackened hearth, the blazing gable's
Telltale cinder where we may
Scorch our shins until that day

We sleepwalk through a No Man's Land
Lipreading to an Orange band.

Continually, therefore we rehearse
Goodbyes to all our characters
And, since both would have it both ways,
On the oily roll of calmer seas
Launch coffin-ship and life-boat,
Body with soul thus kept afloat,
Mind open like a half-door
To the speckled hill, the plover's shore.

So let it be the lapwing's cry
That lodges in the throat as I
Raise its alarum from the mud,
Seeking for your sake to conclude
Ulster Poet our Union Title
And prolong this sad recital
By leaving careful footprints round
A wind-encircled burial mound.[1]

One of the characteristics of the verse-letter is a movement back and forth from the serious to the trivial. That is to say the writer of the verse-letter must maintain the fiction that they are indeed writing a letter, otherwise why bother with the form. A letter is likely to contain material which is trivial to all but the sender and the recipient, but if the author decides not to include that material then the letter will look more like an impersonal essay. Hence writers of verse-letters usually include details which are obviously personal and not of general relevance. In the second line of his letter to Seamus Heaney, Longley tells his friend that he will see him soon, not something which is likely to be of much interest to the reader but which maintains the fiction that what we are reading is, at some level, a personal communication between two people. At the same time, if the letter only includes informal material of this sort then the epistle is in danger of pointlessness. So from the beginning the writer of the verse-letter has to steer a course between matters of general relevance and matters of personal interest. Like many constraints, where poetry is concerned, this is an opportunity.

A further characteristic of the verse-letter is the triangulation between the interests of the speaker, the recipient and the general audience. Like the ode, the epistle encourages the writer to look outside themselves towards other forms of being, or more explicitly in the case of the epistle, another person. Whereas in a lyric poem, the general audience is theoretically present, listening in on the psychological dramas of the poet, the verse-letter behaves differently. Or, to put it another way, a verse-letter cannot be offered like a lyric poem in a take-it-or-leave-it fashion. If it is to seem remotely civilized, it must tailor its speech to the interests of another person. This necessarily makes it difficult to imagine some poets – a poet of obvious interiority like Sylvia Plath, for example – writing a verse-letter.

In the case of Longley's epistle, it is apparent that he has steered it towards a set of preoccupations which he has in common with the recipient, Seamus Heaney. The poem has an obvious informality which is increased by the use of couplets, one of the simplest of technical devices. The poem assumes a familiarity on Heaney's part with a range of landscapes and symbols, some of which a general audience may not be expected to know. Though he comes, like Heaney, from the north of Ireland, Longley makes a point of telling us that he is writing from the west of Ireland, a beautiful, isolated area which contrasts sharply with his troubled province. By drawing a parallel between this retreat and Heaney's experience overseas, Longley reflects on the value of removing oneself from pressing political problems. One advantage of the epistolary form to Longley is that it shows his problems are not his alone, that they may be solved in the social context which the letter helps make possible. Among the other advantages of the form, it gives him an excuse to be topical, in a way that does not admit easy solutions to current problems.

Most letters are directed at the living, but as C. H. Sisson demonstrates in the next poem, many verse-letters are not:

A Letter to John Donne

Note: On 27 July, 1617, John Donne preached at the parish church at Sevenoaks, of which he was rector, and was entertained at Knole, then the country residence of Richard Sackville, third Earl of Dorset.

I understand you well enough, John Donne
First, that you were a man of ability
Eaten by lust and by the love of God
Then, that you crossed the Sevenoaks High Street
As rector of Saint Nicholas:
I am of that parish.

To be a man of ability is not much
You may see them on the Sevenoaks platform any day
Eager men with dispatch cases
Whom ambition drives as they drive the machine
Whom the certainty of meticulous operation
Pleasures as a morbid sex a heart of stone.

That you could have spent your time in the corruption of courts
As these in that of cities, gives you no place among us:
Ability is not even the game of a fool
But the click of a computer operating in a waste
Your cleverness is dismissed from the suit
Bring out your genitals and your theology.

What makes you familiar is this dual obsession;
Lust is not what the rutting stag knows
It is to take Eve's apple and to lose
The stag's paradisal look:
The love of God comes readily
To those who have most need.

You brought body and soul to this church
Walking there through the park alive with deer
But now what animal has climbed into your pulpit?
One whose pretension is that the fear
Of God has heated him into a spirit
An evaporated man no physical ill can hurt.

Well might you hesitate at the Latin gate
Seeing such apes denying the church of God:
I am grateful particularly that you were not a saint
But extravagant whether in bed or in your shroud.
You would understand that in the presence of folly
I am not sanctified but angry.

Come down and speak to the men of ability
On the Sevenoaks platform and tell them
That at your Saint Nicholas the faith
Is not exclusive in the fools it chooses
That the vain, the ambitious and the highly sexed
Are the natural prey of the incarnate Christ.[2]

Like W. H. Auden before him, Sisson directs his epistle to a long-dead poet. Surprisingly perhaps, when compared with a letter to a living person, this alters the effect only slightly. Sisson's poem is centred on the conflict, apparent or otherwise, between the flesh and the spirit, and is openly hostile to those who extol the latter at the expense of the former. He invokes Donne as a kind of fellow-spirit, a religious man of sensual appetites, a figure he can use to compare and contrast with those of his contemporaries of whom he disapproves. In contrast to W. S. Graham's letter to a dead friend, which we will examine shortly, Sisson's poem is addressed to someone that he has never met, and this, interestingly, makes more difference than whether the recipient is alive or not.

Addressing dead writers can have its drawbacks. There is a slight risk, for example, that Sisson's address to Donne may seem presumptuous, that it will look as though he is trying to bathe in the reflected glory of a greater poet. Sisson gets round this problem by avoiding obviously grandiose gestures and by confining his complaints to those of the sensual everyman. He is not too extravagant in his claims to identify with John Donne – he claims, for instance, to understand the dead poet but modifies this statement with the breezy colloquial phrase 'well enough' (without this modification, the opening declaration might seem too stark and really would look presumptuous). Sisson takes the opportunity to triangulate between his own feelings, the presumed attitudes of Donne, and those of the general audience. The advantages of this set of relations is that Sisson appears less alone, advertises that his instincts are decently social, that he wants the best for the other members of his parish, even as he becomes theatrically aggressive about the 'apes' (presumably over-pious clerics) who have hijacked his church. Sisson also takes the opportunity to use diction throughout the letter which is not obviously poetic. Even the rhymes of the poem are relatively muted, so that although the poem is well organized the effect is quite close to that of an average citizen firing off a letter of complaint to a newspaper. Sisson controls the poem by steering carefully between loose slang and excessive formality – the language is relatively natural but avoids being excessively chummy.

In 'Dear Bryan Winter', we find W. S. Graham inventively blending an elegy with some of the peculiar features of the epistle. Especially, Graham exploits the ambiguous one-sidedness of the form, the way in which it directs itself towards another person without having any guarantee of a reply. In this sense, Graham's poem has the uncertainty of a prayer – there is not only the question of whether or not it can be answered, but even the question of whether or not it is heard.

DEAR BRYAN WYNTER

1
This is only a note
To say how sorry I am
You died. You will realise
What a position it puts
Me in. I couldn't really
Have died for you if so
I were inclined. The carn
Foxglove here on the wall
Outside your first house
Leans with me standing
In the Zennor wind.

Anyhow how are things?
Are you still somewhere
With your long legs
And twitching smile under
Your blue hat walking
Across a place? Or am
I greedy to make you up
Again out of memory?
Are you there at all?
I would like to think
You were all right
And not worried about
Monica and the children
And not unhappy or bored.

2
Speaking to you and not
Knowing if you are there
Is not too difficult.
My words are used to that.
Do you want anything?
Where shall I send something?

Rice-wine, meanders, paintings
By your contemporaries?
Or shall I send a kind
Of news of no time
Leaning against the wall
Outside your old house.

The house and the whole moor
Is flying in the mist.

3
I am up. I've washed
The front of my face
And here I stand looking
Out over the top
Half of my bedroom window.
There almost as far
As I can see I see
St Buryan's church tower.
An inch to the left, behind
That dark rise of woods,
Is where you used to lurk.

4
This is only a note
To say I am aware
You are not here. I find
It difficult to go
Beside Housman's star
Lit fences without you.
And nobody will laugh
At my jokes like you.

5
Bryan, I would be obliged
If you would scout things out
For me. Although I am not
Just ready to start out.
I am trying to be better,
Which will make you smile
Under your blue hat.

> I know I make a symbol
> Of the foxglove on the wall.
> It is because it knows you.[3]

As in the other verse-letters we find the characteristic mixture of the informal and the immediate, the inclusion of material which in almost any other kind of poem would look out of place or irrelevant. Graham goes further with these inclusions by making a tension between their informality and the poem's more serious occasion. The opening phrases capture this ambiguity immediately – is it proper for the poet to treat the death of his friend in this mildly humorous fashion? – the opening phrase, for example, cannot do other than draw attention to itself, and the second sentence seems deliberately droll. The details which follow extend this partial joke and it is not until the second section of the poem that Graham offers the reader a justification for what he is doing.

One feature exploited by this verse-letter which we do not find in the other examples is the use of sections. When writing a letter we do not have to write it out at one sitting – we can start it, stop for a bit, resume the next day, or very much later. Therefore it is quite natural for a letter to reflect varied states of mind. This is what we see in Graham's poem. Whereas the first section is almost cheerful in tone – a cheerfulness which perhaps disguises the poet's true feelings – the next section seems to reflect a quite different mood, as though it has been written at another time. This section seems as though it might resolve the puzzling mixture of emotions offered to us in the first, but offers us instead new puzzles, as Graham reflects on the fragile status of his own poems – do we ever communicate successfully in any form of writing? Graham's anxiety about his friend's condition in the afterlife is thereby turned back upon himself. The condition of being alive is brought nearer the condition of death, as though both states offered us only a 'news of no time'. The poet and his dead friend are equalized, for each occupies a lonely space. The sharpness of this shared loneliness is increased as the poet flashes up memories of the pair's good times together. In this sense, the poem draws on another feature of the letter – that it is a hoped-for stay against loneliness, like making a wish that the sender should not be forgotten. It is noticeable that all three verse-letters have running through them a desire for connection, the hope that the author has somebody else on their side.

Your assignment is to write a verse-letter. The poem can be rhymed or unrhymed, but you should aim for a deliberate variousness of tone, and you should try to balance the interests of your addressee with the interests of a general audience.

Notes

1 Michael Longley, *Selected Poems* (London: Cape, 1998), pp. 34–5.
2 C. H. Sisson, *In the Trojan Ditch: Collected Poems & Selected Translations* (Manchester: Carcanet, 1974), pp. 106–7.
3 W. S. Graham, *Selected Poems* (New York: Ecco, 1980), pp. 40–2.

14

The Question of Background

The great detective-fiction writer Raymond Chandler once complained that some of the novels he read did not convey a sense of 'the country behind the hill'. The phrase is suggestive. Chandler's own fiction very much depended on rich and convincing contexts, on the feeling that behind the characters and events he represented lay a complete, living world. In this chapter I want to explore the issue of background, of the country behind every poem's hill. As every poem creates a little world, I want to show how important it is that that world should have depth, the feeling of an independent, breathing life.

Let me offer some analogies from cinema. Sometimes when we watch a film we will be aware that it lacks a convincing hinterland. The street-scenes may seem 'stagey', as though the director has not spent much time thinking what to do about the extras. Or think of those 1950s films in which we see a couple driving along in a car. Very often our attention will slip from their conversation, however fascinating it might be, to the drunken countryside swaying in the window. Poor back-projection can be a distraction. Even films by great directors like Bergman and Hitchcock temporarily suffer from this loss of a persuasive background.

Here is another way of looking at it. Sometimes we will watch a film and be annoyed that the background has been manipulated in such a way as to produce a 'result'. A man we have been watching as he walks down the street is only there, as it turns out, to bump into the lead actor. When a scene looks as if it has been made with a specific agenda in mind, it will make the world of the film feel flat and the film as a whole seem impoverished. One of the things a relatively shallow film will do is seem to reduce the possible kinds of thought there are in the world.

One test of whether or not a poem, novel or film has a convincing background is if you feel that you could walk into its world and imagine its life continuing without the direction of the artist responsible. There are films (about which we might otherwise not think much) like *Star Wars* and *The Lord of the Rings* which redeem themselves with their richly portrayed backgrounds. To offer a small example, in the making of *Star Wars*, one of the early, original ideas was to show high-tech machines in degraded states, spattered with mud, clogged with sand, as though they had individual histories. Here was a film which felt new because it made machines from the future look old.

One of the more easily translated properties of poetry is background – indeed one of the great joys of translated poetry is precisely this quality. Here is a poem by Miroslav Holub which conveys a powerful sense of it:

READING

Before I fell asleep Mother would read me
Jean Christophe, page by page,
like Beethoven falling silent and
a green harp being found. In the fifth part
we finished on page 244.

I went off to fall asleep in another sea,
in another bathyscape.

But Mother no doubt is reading on, somewhere
in the blue room with the picture of breaking waves
in a golden frame, with a cut-glass vase
on the table, with the eye of a young Leviathan at the window,
the hoarse clock on the graveyardlike wardrobe,
the mummies of dictionaries and the skeletons of saltshakers.

She reads in rolling spacetime,
where Notre Dame and Rue Royal Navarin
blend with the rusty little churches in Bohemia
and with the tramcars on Klavotská Street,
where Romain Rolland is an assistant in
Mr Kavan's grocer's shop and Napoleon
assembles his forces to conquer the brewing privilege,

for such is the custom of immortality
of a poet's work, such is the invariant relation
in Mandelbrot's equations,
such is the recreational regime in Hades.

I don't understand what she reads. But when
I awaken I always remember the last
two or three words. And the squeal of the last tramcar
on Klavotská.[1]

As my examples of fantasy films imply, background is not necessarily a matter of realism. Entirely invented worlds may also have this quality – indeed one may argue that they have special *need* of it. Although it conveys a powerful sense of the country beyond 'the last tramcar', Holub's poem is not entirely realistic. Instead, it is a blend of the author's actual childhood world and the fictional world of his mother's reading. The poem persuades us that both the actual and the fictional worlds are real. More importantly, it persuades us that the relationship between the two is real, that one genuinely colours the other, illustrating this beautifully when the mother's words are mingled with the sound of the tramcar.

Background is not just a matter of erecting stage-sets, hastily and haphazardly, in the white space behind characters. It, too, is a matter of relationships. Every character is coloured by their environment, but to have a full sense of an environment we need to watch it work, consistently, on more than one character. Imagine, for a moment, a polar landscape. In the foreground is a man, his dark goggles frosted, his beard hardened with ice. Now further imagine that, in the background, we see others moving around. What those 'extras' are doing will influence our understanding of what the man in the foreground is like. If those others are merely walking along, bundled up in warm clothing, then we will not learn very much – this would be an example of a flat, unimaginative use of background. If, on the other hand, those characters in the background are, say, training dogs, tying fish-hooks or flying kites, we will have an enhanced sense of what it is possible to do in this environment, and therefore an enhanced sense of what sort of character the man in the foreground might be.

Very often, self-absorbed poems do not convey an adequate sense of environment. The speaker may give vent to their feelings – *I love you, I hate you* – but we will have little sense of the force of these feelings because we do not know what the environment makes possible – is this an environment where the speaker falls in love once a lifetime or once a week?

Holub's poem is about himself but it is far from being self-absorbed. We learn about Pilsen, the Czech town from which he hails, not only that it contains churches, tramcars and a brewing privilege, but that these churches and tramcars can be imagined alongside Parisian landmarks, that there is a brewing privilege in Pilsen which can be imagined in the context of Napoleon. Yes, we are looking through the keyhole of Holub's childhood, but it is much more than Holub that we see there.

Here is a portrait of a quite different sort of environment in a poem by the Scottish poet Ian Hamilton Finlay:

ORKNEY INTERIOR

Doing what the moon says, he shifts his chair
Closer to the stove and stokes it up
With the very best fuel, a mixture of dried fish
And tobacco he keeps in a bucket with crabs

Too small to eat. One raises its pincer
As if to seize hold of the crescent moon
On the calendar which is almost like a zodiac
With inexplicable and pallid blanks. Meanwhile

A lobster is crawling towards the clever
Bait that is set inside the clock
On the shelf by the wireless – an inherited dried fish
Soaked in whisky and carefully trimmed

With potato flowers from the Golden Wonders
The old man grows inside his ears.
Click! Goes the clock-lid, and the unfortunate lobster
Finds itself a prisoner inside the clock,

An adapted cuckoo-clock. It shows no hours, only
Tides and moons and is fitted out
With two little saucers, one of salt and one of water
For the lobster to live on while, each quarter-tide,

It must stick its head through the tiny trapdoor
Meant for the cuckoo. It will be trained to read
The broken barometer and wave its whiskers
To Scottish Dance Music, till it grows too old.

> Then the old man will have to catch himself another lobster.
> Meanwhile he is happy and takes the clock
> Down to the sea. He stands and oils it
> In a little rock pool that reflects the moon.[2]

Both Holub and Finlay use a kind of surrealism, in each case with the effect of making their backgrounds seem even more convincing. Finlay's poem presents us with a series of impossibilities, and yet we can feel the way in which the poem depends on the reality of the Scottish island-world from which it arises.

Partly, it is a matter of ingredients. Although it is a poem in which we encounter a man with potatoes growing out of his ears, we sense that everything we see in this space *belongs*. The poem's surrealism has realistic limits. The poem depends on leaving out objects like llamas and coconuts which would not belong in an interior of this sort. It is also a world where the changed details have themselves a kind of 'corrective' quality – it is imaginatively more appropriate that a lobster, rather than a cuckoo, should peek out of an Orkney clock. It is also more appropriate that such a clock should tell the times of the tide rather than the 'actual' time. One might say that the reality of the Orkney background has pushed itself into the speaker's foreground and has set about correcting it.

Notice, too, that this is a portrait of a habitual, almost realistic environment. Everything that happens in the poem looks as though it has happened before, and will keep on happening so long as there are Orkney interiors. In this context, the transformations of the environment seem to grow out of the old man's solitude. We have the sense that the old man is content in this environment but also that he has time on his hands. And in that stretched-out, personal time we can easily imagine him speculating and dreaming in such a way as to see over-familiar objects changing position with each other, as they do in dreams. As in Holub's poem we are made conscious of an exchange between the inside and the outside. In particular it becomes clear that the inside cannot keep the outside out. Just as the squeal of the last tramcar alters the interiority of Holub's home, so the old man is doing 'what the moon says'. The background will not 'stay' back.

The attitude of the speaker in Finlay's poem is not as clear as that of Holub's. What is the relationship between the speaker and the old man? Are they, for example, one and the same? Are they inhabitants of the same village? The coolness of the speaker is itself reassuring, given the improbable situations which he offers us. What we can tell, though, is that the speaker has been immersed in this environment for a tremendous length of time – he presents us with a series of interior relationships which work as well as any well-oiled clock. It would hardly have been possible for the poet to evoke this Orkney life, however idiosyncratic his treatment, without having seen many things which we feel behind, but do *not* see in, the poem.

By way of conclusion, here is a poem of my own in which I deliberately made great play of background. The poem is set in Minnesota, where I spent some years teaching. As an Irish person, I found Minnesota alien and enlivening. The cultural differences were usually sharp, in ways both good and bad. In an attempt to record my mixed feelings about the place I came up with a poem where they rapidly collide:

THE CLOWN LOUNGE

From the Clown Lounge to the Mall of America with love and kisses
– 'Can you pass the CD? It's under your seat' –
From the sole copy of *Fargo* in stock – 'Context?' –
to the SUVs parked on the lake
– 'I can not believe she drives one' –
From wearing shorts all winter
to swallowing bongwater, from walk-in
wardrobes to Kofi on the webpage
from emo-rock and rent-a-wreck
to monster-trucks and ostrich-on-
a-stick – 'There are seats
at the front. You should just come in' –
From Greg's driving – 'I never
hit anything' – to Nick's capture of a traffic-cone
without stopping – 'Don't drive
like my brother!' – From the dead bat
on the department floor – 'Watch out!
It could give you rabies!' – to student
response-sheets – 'Don't set *Self-Portrait in
a Convex Mirror* again. It is bad.' –
From barmen who wear hats
– 'Unless you don't want to come in' –
to the Goths and gamers sitting furthest from the door
– 'Hi! Welcome to our conversation!' –
From the pillar of fire
above an Indian casino – 'Do

you want to come in?' – to the roadsign
approaching Lake George: 'BUMP↓'
From 'Operation Enduring Imperialism'
'I thought it would be a small Chicago . . .' –
to the soccer moms in outer-ring suburbs
– 'but it isn't' – From not getting The Stone
Roses to not getting Ted Hughes
– 'he's too straight for me' – from the wrong
side of the car – 'I'm sorry' –
to the logging-towns which cut down northern Minnesota
– 'and they're *proud* of it!' – from never meeting
a fratboy – 'That works' –
to never meeting a Republican
– 'You should vote for my Dad.
He has a good heart' –
From the secret highway exit for St. Paul
– 'Did I apologize for my driving?' –
to 'the best liberal-arts college in urban Minnesota' –
From Jessica Lange's cheekbones
– 'Could some of your posters not be of white male writers?' –
to a quiet tradition of streakers. From the katydids
that Forrest brought to class
– 'True visionaries don't know the meaning of "no"!' –
to that slow lunar
smudge above the Clown Lounge
– 'Time to dust the sky for fingerprints' – From me
to you, Mac, with hugs and kisses
– 'You should totally come in. Come in.' –
and don't drive like *his* brother.

My intention was to create a collage of my experiences which would present the reader with a variety of impressions. The idea was, first, to throw the reader into the world of Minnesota (much as I had been thrown) and, second, to keep the reader off-balance (much as I had been kept). I wanted the poem to have the genuine tang of the place where I had been, by presenting that world from varied angles, showing it coloured by very different forms of thought. Because I was trying to record a jumble of experiences, there was a considerable danger that the poem would merely be chaotic. Therefore I adopted a structure somewhat in the spirit of a dictum credited to the German poet and philosopher Novalis: 'Chaos in a work of art should shimmer through the veil of order.' The poem creates its veil of order with two major structural principles: parallel phrases based on the formula 'from *x* to *y*'; alternation of those phrases with snatches of conversation. The first principle was suggested to me by the need always to drive in Minnesota, the constant movement from point a to (an entirely different) point b. The second principle was suggested to me by a tension I felt between human voices and their harsh environment.

So this poem never takes time out to say 'Once upon a time I was in Minnesota and here is what I found . . .' There is no conventional attempt to coordinate the impressions and to set out the relationships between them in an easily digestible way. However, I felt that the reader should be able to gather the sorts of experience towards which the poem is pointing. The poem builds up its background with a series of recurrent motifs (driving, college life, cultural misunderstanding) and recurrent tones of voice (the imperative and the interrogative, the kinds of voice which have designs on you). As well as that, the poem indirectly portrays community – or perhaps the absence of community – by referring briefly to a range of groups (goths, visionaries, soccer moms).

The economist Adam Smith famously referred to the workings of the free-market as an 'invisible hand'. A convincing background in a poem is partly conveyed by conveying a sense of forces which are not seen, but which can be felt operating on the details that we *do* see. We might say that a poem with a plausible background has a lot of invisible hands. To take a few examples from 'The Clown Lounge', what is it that influences someone to wear shorts all winter? What is that influences goths and gamers to sit furthest from the door? What is that influences SUVs to park on a frozen lake? Not the same force, you might say, but the reader needs to feel that the kinds of force we find in this particular world – the invisible hands of alienation, individualism, peer pressure, defiance and so on – are working (perhaps to different degrees) on all the images in the poem. If any detail feels like a bad fit, that will probably be because it seems to escape those forces too successfully.

Your assignment is to write a poem with a convincing background. You might want to focus on a world of a kind you know well, so that its workings will seem convincing to the reader. Take the opportunity to let those things which appear in the poem's foreground have lives of their own, to have them act in ways suggested by their environment rather than by what you think you want them to do.

Notes

1 Miroslav Holub, *Supposed to Fly*, trans. Edward Osers (Newcastle: Bloodaxe, 1996), p. 132.
2 Michael Horovitz, ed., *Children of Albion: Poetry of the Underground in Britain*, (Harmondsworth: Penguin, 1969).

15

Conclusion: The Question of Variety

In this concluding chapter, I want to draw some of the threads of the book together. Till now we have looked at themes in relative isolation – what is the effect of having so many voices in a poem, what are the advantages of an unusual viewpoint and so on. In this chapter I want to look at a poem of exceptional richness, 'What The End Is For' by Jorie Graham, to see what happens when a large number of the ideas we have considered are shown at work in the same poem. I have called this chapter 'The Question of Variety' in order to draw attention to the profound flexibility which most great poems share, a deep readiness to move from one very different kind of mood, thought or perspective to another. Throughout this book I have suggested that it is helpful to think of poetry as a relational activity, and to think of a poem as a web of finely drawn relationships. In the case of Jorie Graham's poem, the web is especially fine and bright:

WHAT THE END IS FOR
[GRAND FORKS, NORTH DAKOTA]

A boy just like you took me out to see them,
    the five hundred B-52's on alert on the runway,
fully loaded fully manned pointed in all the directions,
    running every minute
of every day.
    They sound like a sickness of the inner ear,

where the heard foams up into the noise of listening,
    where the listening arrives without being extinguished.

The huge hum soaks up into the dusk.
　　The minutes spring open. Six is too many.
From where we watch,
　　from where even watching is an anachronism,

from the 23rd of March from an open meadow,
　　the concertina wire in its double helix
designed to tighten round a body if it turns
　　is the last path the sun can find to take out,
each barb flaring gold like a braille being read,
　　then off with its knowledge and the sun
is gone . . .

That's when the lights on all the extremities, like an outline, like a dress,
　　become loud in the story,
and a dark I have not seen before
　　sinks in to hold them one
by one.
　　Strange plot made to hold so many inexhaustible
screams.
　　Have you ever heard in a crowd mutterings of
blame

that will not modulate that will not rise?
　　He tells me, your stand-in, they *stair-step* up.
He touches me to have me look more deeply
　　in
to where for just a moment longer
　　color still lives:
the belly white so that it looks like sky, the top
　　some kind of brown, some soil – How does it look

from up there now
　　this meadow we lie on our bellies in, this field Iconography
tells me stands for sadness
　　because the wind can move through it uninterrupted?
What is it the wind
　　would have wanted to find and didn't

leafing down through this endless admiration unbroken
　　because we're too low for it

to find us?
    Are you still there for me now in that dark
we stood in for hours
      letting it sweep as far as it could down over us
unwilling to move, irreconcilable? What *he*
    wants to tell me,

his whisper more like a scream
    over this eternity of engines never not running,
is everything: how the crews assigned to each plane
    for a week at a time, the seven boys, must live
inseparable,
    how they stay together for life,
how the wings are given a life of
    seven feet of play,

how they drop practice bombs called shapes over Nevada,
    how the measures for counterattack in air
have changed and we
    now forego firepower for jamming, for the throwing
of false signals. The meadow, the meadow hums, love, with the planes,
    as if every last blade of grass were wholly possessed

by this practice, wholly prepared. The last time I saw you,
    we stood facing each other as dusk came on.
I leaned against the refrigerator, you leaned against the door.
    The picture window behind you was slowly extinguished,
the tree went out, the two birdfeeders, the metal braces on them.
    The light itself took a long time,

bits in puddles stuck like the useless
    splinters of memory, the chips
of history, hopes, laws handed down. *Here, hold these* he says, these
    grasses these
torn pods, he says, smiling over the noise another noise, *take these*
    he says, my hands wrong for

the purpose, here,
    not-visible-from-the-sky, prepare yourself with these, boy and
bouquet of
    thistleweed and wort and william and

timothy. We stood there. Your face went out for a long time
   before the rest of it. Can't see you anymore I said. *Nor I,*
you, whatever you still were
   replied.
When I asked you to hold me you refused.
   When I asked you to cross the six feet of room to hold me

you refused. Until I
   couldn't rise out of the patience either any longer
to make us
   take possession.
Until we were what we must have wanted to be:
   shapes the shapelessness was taking back.
Why should I lean out?
   Why should I move?
When the Maenads tear Orpheus limb from limb,
   they throw his head

out into the river.
   Unbodied it sings
all the way downstream, all the way to the single ocean,
   head floating in current downriver singing,
until the sound of the cataracts grows,
   until the sound of the open ocean grows and the voice.[1]

This seems to me one of the greatest poems of the late twentieth century, at once profoundly elegant and disturbing. What impresses me most
about the poem is the variety of its thinking, and – although this is no
kind of test of its success – we might usefully apply all of the categories we
have examined in this book to its design. Let us look at these briefly.

The poem has a noticeably complicated manner of *address*. It is spoken
to a boy in a present relationship about a boy in a past relationship. In this
context, note the use of the word 'you', which immediately puts the speaking voice in a dramatic situation. *Viewpoint* is the most powerful of its motifs
and I want to give it extended treatment in a moment. The poem presents
us with a variety of *voices*, from the boy in the past relationship to the boy
in the present one, from Graham as narrator to Graham as a dramatic character speaking both in the past and in the present, from the voice of Orpheus
to the din of the roaring B-52s. There are frequent changes of *scale*, mostly
to reflect shifts in the field of view – we move from 'the last path the sun
can find' to the 'metal braces' of a birdfeeder, from the B-52s dropping

'shapes over Nevada' to a bouquet of wildflowers. The poem uses a great deal of *repetition*, from individual words like 'six' and 'lean', to words repeated at the heads of clauses like 'from' and 'until'. And there are more complicated examples of repetition, like the way in which the bellies of the planes (signalling a pattern of sky below and earth above) relate to the bellies of the lovers (signalling a pattern of earth below and sky above). The poem's *imagery* is functionally vivid. Consider how the passage of time is associated with images of diminishing light, and consider, too, how the image of the planes in outline appearing like a dress neatly draws together the military and domestic contexts of the poem. As a structuring principle the poem relies on the interlacing *long and short lines* – and while this allows for numerous verbal effects, one should also note how it mimics, in a rough visual way, the '*stair-step*' of the planes, just as the expansion and contraction of the lines mimics the expansion and contraction of the various points of view. The *diction* of the poem moves skilfully between words of different register, from 'timothy' to 'counterattack', from runs of simple monosyllables (like the first line) to the use of unusual polysyllables like 'shapelessness' and 'Unbodied'. The *syntax* is carefully varied, from the colloquially elliptical 'Can't see you' to lengthy sentences with parallel clauses, like the one which begins, 'What *he* wants to tell me . . .'. The poem's *tone* is very various, at different times affectionate, passionate, puzzled, wistful, speculative, frightened, and many shades in between. As far as *background* is concerned, we are given a very deep impression of the environments which the speaking voice brings to our attention, from the fine texture of the meadow to the grainy light in the kitchen. The reader comes away from the poem with the feeling that the B-52s are still roaring on that airfield. And while it would be stretching matters to claim that this poem is formally equivalent either to an *ode* or an *epistle*, it does share some of the qualities of these poems – the dramatically immediate, public form of address and the deliberate movement out of the self towards another person ('I asked you to cross the six feet of room to hold me').

Of all the categories we might bring to bear, the poem makes most play of *viewpoint*, moving back and forth from an expansive outdoors field of view to a narrow, domestic one. Viewpoint is not just a means of organizing the material in the poem, it is a part of the poem's material. Principally, there are two fields of view – one is the view of the planes arranged on the airfield; the other the view which the two pairs of lovers have of each other. In each case the poem foregrounds the act of watching. In this context, note the way in which relatively little actually *happens* in the poem.

Much of the poem's energy seems to derive not from what is happening, but from thinking about what might happen in the future – the planes might embark on a mission, the lovers might suddenly embrace. The various options are kept in view. Of course any point of view is self-consciously relational, and see how careful Graham is to describe the relative positions of objects and people – 'we stood facing each other', 'How does it look // from up there now'. From the end of the second stanza to the beginning of the third, she piles up a number of simultaneous viewpoints. In the face of the bombers arranged on the airfield, Graham suggests that she is looking 'from where even watching is an anachronism' – and this might make us think about the technological means at the disposal of the pilots, the hardware and software which help them to fly without seeing (in a moral as well as physical sense). The suggestion of anachronism is picked up by the later reference to Iconography, a way of reading visual information which seems out of date but which is deliberately used to contrast with the more modern pilot's viewpoint. So one way of reading this poem is as a competition *between* viewpoints, those which seem resolutely contemporary and those which seem outmoded. In the face of the awesome military power of the aeroplanes, the point of view of the lovers is made to seem fragile, almost like a thing of the past. And the poem also invites us to think about what cannot be seen – that which cannot be viewed from a particular perspective – to which Graham draws attention with the phrase 'not-visible-from-the sky'. Perhaps the poem's most formidable achievement is the way in which it sets up so many energetic parallels between the different types of viewpoint. It is instructive how Graham wastes no energy in her description but sets up connections which in each case work powerfully on the reader. To take a few examples, the 'seven feet of play' is paralleled with the six feet between the lovers (and there is a suggestion here, too, of six feet under), the wings of the B-52s are paralleled with the metal braces of the birdfeeder, the first romantic relationship with the second, the close family relationship of the pilots with the awkward conclusion of a love affair. So intricate is the design that one can't experience one part of the poem without feeling its influence on another part. It is a honeycomb of viewpoints.

I do not want to pretend that writing a great poem like this is easy. Rather, by considering how many different elements are in play, I want to suggest how difficult it can be. A great poem is not the result of performing a few cunning technical tricks. Rather it is produced by a harmonious integration of as many different elements of the author's personality as possible.

A poem like this can only by written by a personality held open to an unusual range of influences, with the energy to draw connections between them, and the faith not to let those connections go stiff. Novalis said that chaos, in a work of art, should always shimmer behind the veil of order. A poem like this can only be written by a personality prepared to shape its thinking, over and over, against the shapelessness.

Note

1 Jorie Graham, *The Dream of the Unified Field: Selected Poems* (Manchester: Carcanet, 1996), pp. 66–9.

Index

Lightning Source UK Ltd.
Milton Keynes UK
UKOW021051050112

184794UK00002B/57/P